MISERABLY SUCCESSFUL NO MORE

MISERABLY SUCCESSFUL NO MORE

POWER OVER STRESS

DEBJANI MUKHERJEE BISWAS

Edited by • Performance Publishing Group • Ellen Linden
• Niket Biswas
Cover Design by Performance Publishing Group
BACC Support • Sandra Hoffman • Linda Smittle
• Barbara Weinberger
Published by Performance Publishing Group March 2017

ISBN 13: 978-1-946629-12-8 (sc)
ISBN 10: 1-946629-12-X (sc)
ISBN 13: 978-1-946629-13-5 (hc)
ISBN 10: 1946629-13-8 (hc)
ISBN 13: 978-1-946629-14-2 (e)
ISBN 10: 1-946629-14-6 (e)

Because of the dynamic nature of the Internet, any web addresses or links contained in this book may have changed since publication and may no longer be valid.

FIRST EDITION

Global Impact Statements Include:

Austria - "A brilliant and very inspirational woman."
~ *Cornelia Kalcher Tsuha, Founder of Global Success Coaching*

Australia - "Learning from her ideas influences my thinking in powerful ways."
~ *Andrea Dean*

Canada - "Debjani Biswas is an excellent communicator and demonstrates a real commitment to supporting change."
~ *Alison Hendren, MCC, CEO of Coaching out of the Box*

Finland - "An inspirational role model. She contributes to making the world a better place."
~ *Kshama Motha*

Germany - "A female engineer who spent two decades in corporate America — tremendously authentic impressions, ideas, advice."
~ *Ladislaus V. Daniels*

Japan - "I believe Debjani Biswas is living and walking diversity."
~ *Susumu Araki, CEO Global Management Development Inc.*

El Salvador & USA - "A new, out of the box perspective, using a unique 'engineering principles approach' — a set of very practical tools."
~ *Mario Bolanos, Director WRAE*

Nigeria - "The first word that comes to mind is 'brilliant.' An inspiration."
~ *Ronke Okpa, PMP*

Thailand - "Inspired guidance and a practical toolkit. You'll find yourself examining options to improve everyday interactions."
~ *Linda Smittle, Peace Corps Volunteer*

United Kingdom - "What I particularly like is the combination of practical insights (as a former executive of a Fortune 50 company) and an engineering background, applied to original frameworks to solve emotional, business related issues."
~ *David Taylor, Managing Partner The Sense of Group*

United States - "A woman of amazing intelligence, managerial courage and strategic vision."
~ *Barbara Weinberger, Principal Weinberger Consulting[1]*

**Caminante, No Hay Camino
Se Hace Al Andar.**

Translation:
Walker, there is no path.
The path is made by walking.

~ Antonio Machado

This book is dedicated to our authentic,
generous and talented son Niket Biswas—
one of the finest human beings I know.
The gift of being your mother keeps on giving.

Thanks to family who are also friends,
and friends who feel like family.

"We'll bleed and fight for you – We'll make it right for you
If we lay a strong enough foundation
We'll pass it on to you, we'll give the world to you
And you'll blow us all away."
Lin Manuel Miranda-Hamilton

Table of Contents

Section Four:
Miserably Successful No More!

Preface

Why Being Miserably Successful
No More Matters

In 2012, I was suddenly laid off from an excellent job. Though shocked to the core, being laid off was the best thing that could have happened. Being pushed out of this door forced another one to open, leading me to an excellent place. Not only am I miserably successful no more, *my life today is just — better.* Much better, in the ways that count.

There is a global epidemic of the miserably successful. Perhaps misery is too strong for you. You are just stressfully successful. You appear fine outwardly, **yet die a little inside each day.** Trapped in an unhappy — yet highly paid — autopilot existence. This book is designed to make you stop, as I was forced to, and take time to become mindful of who you really are and what you can achieve.

Three observations caused me to write this book:

1. *We create much of our own stress* by ignoring our authentic style — introvert or extravert, assertive or mild, measured or quick.
2. *Amazing improvement is possible* from *tiny, courageous choices* to be perfectly imperfect and speak, and live, our truth.

3. These choices depend upon a powerful vision: *a laser sharp focus and direction.*

When applied with purpose, these shifts can lead to peace, reduced stress, greater purpose. I grew up happy but, somewhere along the way, became a miserably successful version, stressed out, fearful, always running. Bronnie Ware[2], an Australian nurse, reported the "Top Five Regrets of the Dying" in a blog called "Inspiration and Chai." These were the regrets:

1. I wish I'd had **the courage to live a life true to myself, not the life others expected of me.**
2. I wish I hadn't worked so hard.
3. I wish I'd had **the courage to express my feelings.**
4. I wish I had stayed in touch with my friends.
5. I wish that I had **let myself be happier.**

How do we jumpstart the way back to letting ourselves be happier? First, we *stop lying to ourselves* and others. Next we cut through the clutter and *stop doing* irrelevant things. Then we *start doing* what we were meant to do and excel at.

What would happen if we applied *an engineering mindset of data harvesting and pattern recognition to behavioral differences?*

Driving in my car, happily exhausted after speaking for hours on this topic, a thought pops into my mind. I have enough. Physically, financially, emotionally, spiritually, intellectually. At this moment, I experience equanimity. *Peace settles inside my car, like drifting snowflakes, curling into the sides, swirling as it lands into the stillness of my heart.* I am reminded of a quote: "Now and then, it is good to pause in our pursuit of happiness...and just be happy." This book is, therefore, also my gift to you. A way of saying thank you for picking up the pieces and dusting me off when I fell to the floor, in an explosion of professional and personal crises.

Here are the key principles, collated as uncomfortable, stark truths:

- We, who are otherwise scrupulously honest, **lie to ourselves**, often, about our stress and well-being levels, while suppressing our dreams and hopes.
- We, who are so kind to our friends and families, show *ourselves* no, or little, respect or kindness.
- We fill our lives with so much stuff that we lose focus and stop thinking with clarity and direction.

Read this book with an open mind. Recognize, and leverage your unique style to improve authentic success and well-being. Redefine success so your life revolves around more than money and prestige alone. Recognize the choices you make to self-sabotage, then apply practical tools to stop doing these things. Along the way, *learn to power over stress, listening to the melody of your emerging life song*; so, together, we can be miserably successful no more.

Section One

Introduction

This section outlines how to navigate easily through the book, plus the importance of understanding the global epidemic of the miserably successful.

We explore two questions:

- Why are you reading a book entitled *Miserably Successful No More*?
- What is your vision or purpose in life?

Chapter 1

A Door Slams Shut

"I'm sorry but you have been laid off." Gavin's office was tastefully appointed, with pictures of his family, original artwork, an elegant vase with fresh flowers. No, wait, focus. This was important. He was saying something really important; but it just didn't make sense. The Human Resources manager sitting next to him was looking at me, with a worried look in his kind eyes. Why did this feel like an out of body experience? The words floated through the air, some entering conscious thought, others escaping through the windows to the woods below. Phrases swirled: "it was a difficult decision...a number of executives impacted in your demographic...do you have any questions...will you sign this document within the next few days..."

Our CEO's speech on "flattening the organization" and "investing more on advertising" had driven a stake through my career and future. It felt like swimming underwater, moisture in my ears: muffled, heavy, a rushing sound. How could this have happened to me? I had survived two decades in global organizations and was now an executive at a Fortune 50 corporation. In 2009, when three quarters of my team was impacted, I had escaped the dreaded list.

"This must have been difficult for you. Really appreciate your concern." I could hear the words coming from my mouth, and both the leaders visibly relaxed. Telegraphing that this would not escalate, no need to call Employee Assistance or Security, always on hand for events like this. How did I know this? Unfortunately, I had experience delivering these messages to others, from the opposite end of the table.

So, this was what it felt like: why Jennifer Davidson (name changed for anonymity) dropped her keys three times in two minutes after receiving a similar message. Why she told us her husband was out of town, and she had never, once, received a *does not meet expectations* rating, as she cried silently, dry tears, bewildered, almost glued to her chair.

I, Debjani Biswas, had been let go; rejected, discarded, rendered obsolete. Slowly, I walked back to the office. One of my direct reports was waiting with a sad face. Bad news travels fast. The HR Manager assigned to my case knocked on the door. "If you have anything to download before handing me your laptop, please do so now. You don't have to pack up your things right away. When would you like to return and clear out your office?"

"Over the weekend," I whispered. Fewer people to see my shame, the voice inside agreed. My phone pinged: a reminder for lunch with my ex-boss and lifelong mentor. *Should I reschedule? No. Leave now, go to the car. Look around, think. Is there something here that you don't want them to see as they pack your boxes?*

My office neighbor and good friend stood by the door. "So sorry to hear the news, Debjani. Can I help in any way?" I replied, pleasantly, calmly, as if nothing was wrong, "Thank you, no, nothing. Appreciate the offer, though."

An hour later, I quietly picked up my purse, phone and empty laptop bag. Scurrying down the corridor to the car, the term 'walk of shame' finally made sense. I sat in the car for about fifteen minutes. "It will be OK," an inner voice said. "Will it really?" Challenged another voice. *"No. This is the end."*

"Last night as I was sleeping,
I dreamt—marvelous error!—
that I had a beehive
here inside my heart.
And the golden bees
were making white combs
and sweet honey
from my old failures."

Antonio Machado

Chapter 2

New Beginnings – An Exploration

> **Stress has been a constant companion:**
> **like a dirty windshield, obstructing**
> **and marring even the most**
> **magnificent view ahead.**

This chapter explores two fundamental concepts:

- Where you want to go — your vision.
- The Three-Legged Stool — your current support system's stability.

I will share some of my experiences following the layoff in order to make these concepts come to life for you.

Developing a Vision: In the months that followed, I went through the predictable stages of change[3]. The numbness continued for many days. I cycled between resistance and denial, anger and shock. An odd cocktail of embarrassment, shame, bravado and boldness, with rare glimpses of exhilarating freedom and new avenues. And slowly, very slowly, crawled into exploration and the occasional glimpse of possibilities, an exciting hopefulness.

My son asked me a deceivingly simple question, "For years you have been talking about writing a book. What are you waiting for?" This simple question had no compelling response. I decided to follow a path untraveled, exploring the world of speaking and writing. My first major event was at the International Coach Federation Global Conference in London, addressing business professionals from 23 countries and many languages. After the session (on reducing bias using a practical global toolkit) people clustered around, asking for autographs on conference brochures. Their heartfelt support signaled that the message: unity through diversity — of style, culture, gender, generation — meant something.

Let's pause here. It took a traumatic life-changing event for me to rethink my path. I was almost *forced* to develop a vision. You don't have to go through a career crisis or a life-changing event to answer the question. Do you have a vision? If so, is it compelling enough to powerfully shape your behaviors? Some people get stuck when facing adversity, others find the grit and resilience to emerge stronger on the other side. A lot depends on one's support systems when life knocks us down. We will explore The Three-Legged Stool of stability in a minute. But first, please write down *your vision, with as much detail* around it as you can articulate.

Author's Note: Record your vision in the appendix section. To honor diverse preferences, there are blank pages (for less structured reflection and action planning) as well as structured worksheets. A few topics have worksheets embedded in the text also.

Coming back to that moment, I experienced what Neuro Linguistic Programming (NLP) master practitioner Lane Pierce calls future memories. This is a very powerful tool I want you to practice.

When you finalize your vision (perhaps you already have one), imagine *precisely* what it looks like.

- What does this moment feel like?
- What exactly are you doing?
- What are you wearing?
- What are you holding in your hand?
- Where is this happening (location)?

Make a vivid movie in your mind, and play it over and over again. This tool is incredibly powerful; it can drag you through the drudgery of the difficult things that make glamorous goals achievable. I could see, feel and almost taste it. The conviction that one day there would be a book in my hand, autographed and handed over to a participant, just like this one.

Fast forward again, July 2013: a knock on the door, a package. Fingers trembling, I tore open the tape and binding, and gently, reverently, pulled out the first copy of *Unleash the Power of Diversity*. As I took it to the framed photograph of my late father and said Durga Durga[4] (my culture's equivalent to 'bless this'), I was shocked to see an obvious anomaly in the cover page.

From the sublime to the ridiculous, with emotions jumping all over the place...instantly transported back to the stressful place that is so familiar. Self-doubt reared its ugly head with familiar questions: "How could you be so stupid — what were you thinking?" Voices of past critics played in my mind, comparing me negatively to others, memories of past failures getting stronger.

And in that instant, a shift took place. A feeling of peace, of equanimity, of inner self. The finished work product of a year was a reality, and it had gone through a nightmarish six months of editing and formatting. There had been moments of such frustration that the project almost died. We dug, battered and powered our way through it anyway. My son's words echoed in the background. "Enjoy every minute, for you will never get a second chance to experience what writing a first book feels like." I experienced a deep sense of satisfaction and the realization that *none of this would have been possible if I had not been laid off*. A surprising and powerful learning point.

Gently, I placed the book in front of my late father's picture and took a photograph. Every moment, the vision: "Learning, helping, teaching with graceful flawed authenticity" comes a step closer. A series of books on four key aspects of Diversity: Culture, Style, Gender and Generation.

You picked up this book because you understood the phrase "miserably successful." You may have laughed and said, "I am successful but not miserable. Just stressed out some times." Or "Thank goodness I am happily unsuccessful — a choice I made." Or, a little more honestly, you may have said to someone else, "This describes me perfectly." It doesn't matter. The fact is you picked it up. And you, like me, are a work in progress.

A combination of events rocked my world at the core: professional (the layoff) and personal (potentially life threatening health issues). Struggling through the grief and shock, there was a desperate need for purpose and sanity in my life. For the next two months, I embarked on a journey of self-discovery to arrive at the vision *"Learning Helping Teaching - with Graceful Flawed Authenticity."*

What is your vision—and does it inspire you toward the life you deserve?

Close your eyes for at least a minute. See, vividly, how your life is today. The beautiful patches, the not so pretty, the hidden, the empty. What would it be like if you weren't so stressed, so often? Now, open your eyes slowly. Think about a vision, a dream, a "one day I wish" statement you made to yourself, yesterday or decades ago. Decide if you are afraid of your own greatness, or will do what it takes to be the best version of yourself. How do we operationalize this visualizing technique?

<u>**Author's Note**</u>: There is an inspirational photograph of a pivotal event in front of me as a reminder that editing this manuscript — not my forte — is part of the vision. Experience severe frustration, suddenly realizing I am editing an older version! Remind myself that professional editing follows, and regain perspective.

The Three-Legged Stool - Stability of Support Systems

Before "boldly going where no human has before"[5] we will assess the stability of our intertwined support systems. Like a Three-Legged Stool, we need at least two to be strong. I was able to make radical changes because, while my internal leg was wobbling, the other two legs stood firm until balance was restored.

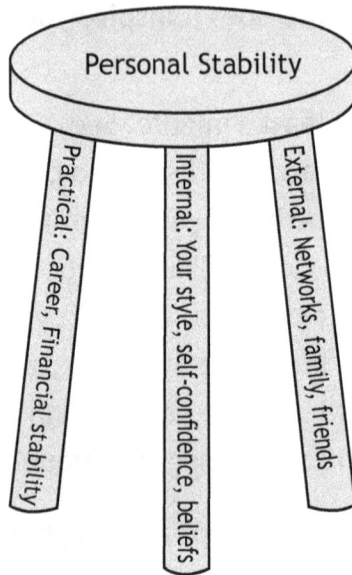

Figure 1: The Three-Legged Stool - Stability of Support Systems

The three types of support are:

Practical: Career, financial stability, professional life, avocation. This is, of course, relative to an individual's monetary needs and obligations.

Internal: You, your style, personality, abilities, skills, strength of character, integrity, personal power and self-confidence.

External: Networks, including family, friends, strategic alliances, business colleagues, sponsors, leaders, professional organizations.

Rate where you are now on each of these three legs (using a one to ten scale if useful to you). Next, go back to a period that is significant to you, comparing your numbers then and now.

<u>Author's Note</u>: As with all the reflections in the book, do this mentally or in the appendix pages, as suited to your information processing style.

When you start following your vision, reducing stress, doing more of the things that increase your well-being, your balance is critical. Identify your strongest sources of support here, and we will assess danger zones later. Determine practical aspects of your finances, set appropriate guard rails for peace of mind. Money shouldn't be an obsession, but knowing you have 'enough' (if that is accurate) is a huge gift. Enough may be less than you thought: analyze current life choices, which may be misaligned with your values. *Do you have to buy or lease a luxury car every three years because one of your direct reports has one?*

I am making assumptions here: that you are financially comfortable if you are reading a book called *Miserably Successful No More*. That may or may not be accurate. If the latter, then of course Maslow's Hierarchy of Needs[6] applies. We can't go to self-actualization until we have a roof over our heads and ongoing food and electricity. Physical support is the first thing that must be in place for our Three-Legged Stool to be stable.

Finally, how will you navigate this book most effectively? The book is divided into sections, focusing on what is making us miserable, how we define happiness and success, things we can stop doing to free up precious energy, skills we can build to get what we really want from life. The most effective way is to read it through, then go back to critical sections and action plan.

If stress is a major factor in your life right now, focus on that first. Stress makes intelligent, otherwise sensible people behave foolishly and self-destructively. Chronic stress can, over time, even be life threatening. Hopefully you will recognize and break your unproductive stress cycles. Once you realize how you are getting in your own way, you can refocus and re-frame. Am I able to write so much about stress because I am so good at managing it? Not at all. I was ill equipped, by both nature and nurture, to handle the pressures of life, and have suffered greatly as a result. For decades. *Stress has been a constant companion: like a dirty windshield, obstructing and marring even the most magnificent view ahead.* My head has known it; my mind has felt powerless to deal with it.

Together, we can do, be, learn, give back, help, experience...*so much*. You are not alone on this journey.

Section Two

Who Are You? - Foundational Tools and Skill Building

This section focuses on self-awareness and skill building, customized to your unique style, recognizing others' different personality and behavior traits.

We discuss both traditional and original style diversity tools:

- Emotional Intelligence – The Reuven Bar-On Model
- Two Truths and a Lie: An Original Communication Style Self-assessment
- The Five Judgments – A Bias and Stereotyping Framework

Chapter 3

Foundational Concepts

*Communication occurs when the messages
we send are understood and received.*
Effective interactions, therefore, are not
just about content, they are about
content and process.

In the first section, the discussion focused on the case for action: the importance of reducing stress, recognizing the toll of being miserably successful. I asked if you had a compelling vision, and whether you were moving purposefully toward it. This section is about self-awareness: your personality as it relates to others, and how your style works for, or against you. The foundational concepts and skill building tools in this section are:

- Emotional Intelligence – Self-awareness and Interpersonal Skills
- Two Truths and a Lie – an Original Tool on Diverse Communication Styles
- Style Norms – a Self-assessment on Deep-Rooted Style Values and Norms

- The Five Judgments – a Framework on Style Biases and Stereotypes

Style diversity skill building is based upon Emotional Intelligence. *First, we understand our individual preferences, next we realize how we relate to others who are different from us.* We are born with a certain set of behavioral characteristics, and develop strong beliefs about the value of these, and opposing behaviors in others. These are right versus wrong judgments. By using pattern recognition and data harvesting we can uncover, as the true experts of ourselves, who we really are. In this chapter, we will explore Emotional Intelligence and communication styles.

Emotional Intelligence

Emotional Intelligence (EI) is a composite of how we see and express ourselves individually, relate to others, make decisions and handle stress. There is an ongoing, heated debate between technologists and behavioral professionals about the importance of EQ (Emotional Quotient) versus IQ (Intelligence Quotient). There is a fundamental difference between emotional and traditional intelligence. IQ relates to academic skills, book smarts, functional competence in technical areas and testing abilities. A person may be – and often is – both emotionally immature and brilliant. For example, a technically competent person may struggle in project funding because of arrogance and a poor relationship with her boss.

Why is Emotional Intelligence so critical to being miserably successful no more? We interact with others every day. Awareness of our emotional responses and how we relate to others, particularly under pressure, helps us change both the process and content of our story.

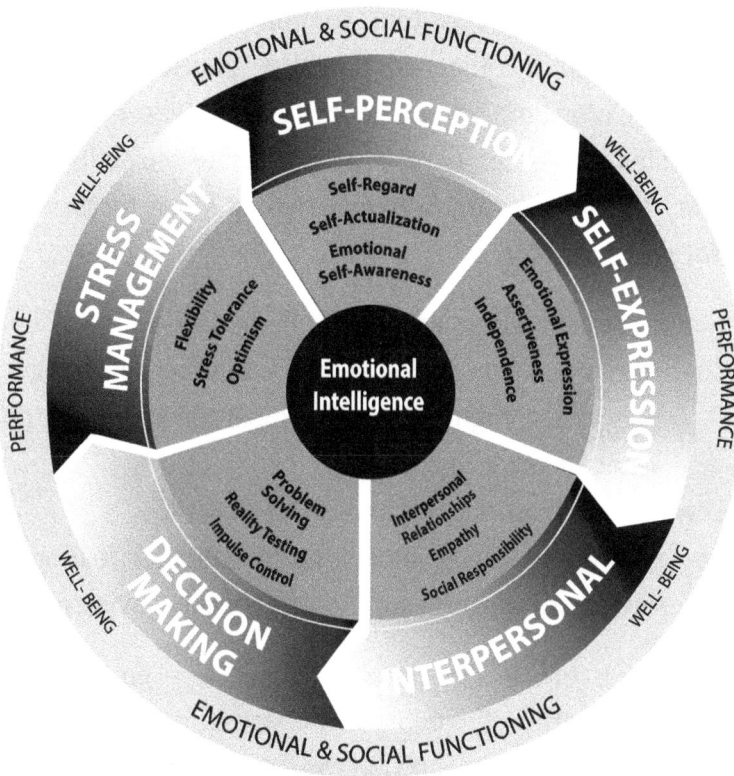

Figure 2: Emotional Intelligence Framework - Reuven Bar-On Model

Summary of Key Emotional Intelligence Composites

Self-Perception: Self-Regard, Self-Actualization, Emotional Self-Awareness

Self-Expression: Emotional Expression, Assertiveness, Independence

Interpersonal: Interpersonal Relationships, Empathy, Social Responsibility

Decision Making: Problem Solving, Reality Testing, Impulse Control

Stress Management: Flexibility, Stress Tolerance, Optimism

This framework is an excellent summary of the key concepts around Emotional Intelligence. Ideally, please take the self-assessment at mhs.com, or self-identify areas where you exercise these muscles more than in other areas. While the skills alone are important, *the interaction between two or more factors is more powerful and practical.*

- High in assertiveness and low in flexibility?
  - o If in a position of power, you could be enforcing a 'my way or the highway' leadership style so people don't want to work for you.
- Low in assertiveness and high in flexibility?
  - o You may be saying yes to a lot of things for fear of repercussions, instead of courageously saying no.

A person who is low in Emotional Intelligence — particularly self-awareness, empathy, flexibility and stress tolerance — often struggles with pattern recognition, adaptation and growth. There is also a multiplier effect: lack of self-awareness often equals low learning agility. Remaining authentic while fitting into a new environment requires social awareness, which is a key component of Emotional Intelligence.

Which three EQ muscles do you exercise most often, and which three the least? We all have certain behavioral tendencies: recognizing that our strengths, overused, can turn into weaknesses is the first step. Impatient listening is my challenge, linked to high assertiveness. The flip side is the positive aspect of that trait: getting things done quickly.

Two Truths and a Lie — An Original Style Diversity Communication Tool

We expand our self-discovery with a communication style assessment that I titled *Two Truths and a Lie*. This gauges how blunt versus indirect we are, particularly in moments of tension or conflict. The title is designed to jolt awareness: being too polite and nice is a lie sometimes; the same way that blurting out the unvarnished truth can destroy relationships and people.

What is your innate Two Truths and a Lie preference?

Each of us has a natural tendency toward bluntness or softness: understanding this diversity of style is critical. First, to understand the value of the opposing style. Second, to adjust our response for more effective communication. In interactions, *particularly, where there is tension, conflict, differences of opinion or unmet needs*, most of us tend toward one of three responses.

1.   The Blunt Truth
2.   The Palatable Truth
3.   The Glossy Lie

Hence the phrase – two truths and a lie.

1.   ***The Blunt Truth*** – teller uses the hammer approach: the truth, the plain truth, and nothing but the truth. The advantage of the hammer approach is trust: what you see is what you get: the hammer is real. She is the canary in the coal mine, she tells it like it is. The hammer is usually respected for her courage. The disadvantage: hammers can be bullies, hurt

people's feelings, leave body bags, have low followership and be disliked or actively avoided.

2. *The Palatable Truth* – teller combines honesty with kindness. He is able to give the news of positives and negatives about the situation or the person, without resorting to mean spirited 'honesty'. His courage and unselfishness — not having to be right all the time — enables him to develop deep, true relationships without leaving body bags behind him. This involves skillful use of Emotional Intelligence skills such as empathy, assertiveness, flexibility, stress tolerance.

3. *The Glossy Liar* – is like a paint brush: agrees with everything we say, tells us that we are great, that all is well. Sometimes, he does this because of fear that people will see him for 'the impostor that he is' (in his mind). So, in order to be liked or loved, he is a people pleaser; saying what he thinks others want to hear. Some glossy liars will also whisper negative things about you behind your back. The glossy liar is usually liked; can be pitied, invisible, mistrusted, disrespected.

Obviously each extreme style has positives and negatives. *Communication occurs when the messages we send are understood and received.* Effective interactions, therefore, are not just about content, they are about context and process.

Some important considerations include style preference, our history, the stress each of us is under, the state of mind the receiver is in: how much kindness he needs, how much honesty he can take. Personality, power, stress and cultural norms also impact every interaction. Safety matters: if a person doesn't enjoy conflict, and the person in power, e.g. parent or boss, is critical and judgmental; it feels safer to gloss over the truth. Conversely, a safe, high trust, mutually respectful, relationship makes it easier to be blunt. Leveraging situation specific approaches and tools, after a quick multivariate analysis, lets us become nimble in diverse communications.

We can use the blunt truth without toxic results, in high trust relationships, though it must be used sparingly, or else it abuses this trust. Most of us lack the skill to be totally honest without being hurtful, so we leave out critical facts; this is not ideal either. Are you actually speaking the entire truth: or *glossing over important things*, conveniently *choosing to share inconsequential truths*? Over time, white lies build up like a disease, causing you more stress, eroding your respect in yourself. On the other extreme, when we misuse the hammer style, using cruelty disguised as honesty: we alienate others: hammers typically have more enemies than brushes.

Do more people like you, or respect you? Both are important. Which one does your behavior drive? What would it take for you to shoot straight and deliver negative feedback and keep the relationship strong? For most of us, speaking the palatable truth takes time, skills and practice.

Now let's make the *Two Truths and a Lie* instrument come alive with an example.

Scenario: Dinner Party

Background Information: The hostess has invited 16 friends for a home cooked dinner. She has taken the day off to cook, and the room is tastefully appointed. When you take a bite of the fried fish that she said was so difficult to make, you almost choke. It is too salty and quite inedible! At that moment, your hostess stops by, and noticing that you are eating the fish, asks "How do you like the fish?"

Here are some examples, operationalizing the *Two Truths and a Lie* spectrum of responses.

- *__Blunt Truth:__* It's too salty and dry — I don't like it.
- *__Glossy Lie:__* It's wonderful! I love it!
- *__Palatable Truth:__* I really appreciate the effort you put into hosting so many of us today.

What are your first instincts? We tend to land on one or the other extreme, intrinsically. Most people have a self-serving bias and immediately self-identify as being palatable truth sayers.

> **If we understand the why of our behavior (fear of_____) and combine it with the how (*five ways to say yes*), the behavior change can be powerful.**

There is obviously a cultural aspect to this. I am climbing up a slippery slope of generalization with this next statement. After having lived in both the Americas and Asia, my impression is that white lies are labeled social necessities in the US; being blunt is more acceptable in much of Europe and Asia. Some business functions also lean toward one or the other: Operations, Finance and Engineering are more fact based and blunt; Sales, Marketing, Public Relations are more polished and indirect. Who amongst us hasn't seen a hairdresser gushing about someone's lovely hair when, in fact, that person's hair is sparse or unattractive? Between males and females, men tend to be more direct than females. Of course, there are direct (aggressive, even!) females and indirect, euphemistic males. I am talking about percentages, not absolutes.

Self-awareness and Skill Building:

So, what shall we do with this data about our communication style?

For a month, observe yourself in multiple interactions and see which of the three communication styles you lean toward. Don't judge, or even try to correct, just observe.[7] Mentally rehearse what the three options (or more) could have been, especially in sticky situations. It's easy to be pleasant when both parties agree. What happens to your normal responses under stress or conflict? In these interactions, reflect on what another response could have been. All casually, in a nonjudgmental way. For example, if you are always blunt in talking about something, and declaring proudly "That's who I am", follow the data. Are fewer and fewer people reaching out to you to partner on projects? Are you willing to try something a little different for at least one of the next ten interactions?

While staying authentic to yourself, can you move toward use of the palatable truth? What is your purpose in being brutally candid every time? Why is keeping the relationship not a consideration for you? Is your truth a crutch, an excuse for hurting others in the name of honesty?

You may be surprised at how often you don't voice the truth, when you try this exercise. You may have fooled yourself into thinking that this doesn't happen often. Try this for a month. Just thinking, mindfully, about what you really feel about this situation, and what you really want to say. Obviously the glossy brush would really benefit from practicing this technique, and so also would some hammers.

No judgment. No 'but I shouldn't feel this way, that's unreasonable, ungrateful'... Just respect and be aware of what the true thoughts are in your mind. Every time there is a twinge of tension, make a note of that also. Is the tension higher because I agreed verbally and didn't really want to? Or because I disagreed and noticed a frown on the other person's face which I interpreted to be disapproval of my action?

Just be aware. And then, if you are prepared, and have developed some level of skill, try this. See what happens if you say what you mean, exactly as you mean it, for something very low risk, with someone who is either an ally or very approachable. Definitely don't practice on your boss or someone in power the first time. Again, remember these are suggestions, to be applied with common sense and caution. Don't do anything to jeopardize your success or career, obviously.

For me, speaking my mind was liberating beyond belief. The transition that I experienced from people pleaser (brush) to overly blunt person (hammer) to, hopefully palatable truth teller (glue gun) took decades. Of course, the pendulum swung too far the first few times I tried to change. Though it cost me in relationships and resources, the trade off has been worth it.

Now let's come to you. Are you willing to try something new? If so, let us also combine this technique (self-awareness about what you really think) with the tactical tool *Five Ways to Say Yes* (see page 73). If we understand the why of our behavior (fear of_____) and combine it with the how (Five Ways to Say Yes), the behavior change can be powerful. Just looking, calmly, without judgment, at your calendar will tell you a lot. First, how to refocus if you are not spending your time on what's really important. Second, that even within a schedule as tight as yours might be, there are ways to build in breathing space. What is one simple thing you can do to recenter yourself in a frantically busy time? It may be a surprisingly trivial solution.

This book is about style diversity. About recognizing what is natural and life-saving for your unique style. It is about honoring who you are inside, regardless of the tired stereotypes you have harbored for years, maybe decades, of who you should be. As you read this example, start jotting down the simple solutions that will reduce your stress during high volume, high pressure pockets of time in your life. Let me give you a concrete example: Arriving the night before a keynote is a simple tool I use wherever possible. After several flight delays, there was a very stressful event where I literally walked into the banquet hall and started speaking, without breakfast or lunch. So I arrive the night before: strategic buffering for critical events has a positive benefit-cost ratio.

> This book is about style diversity.
> About recognizing what is natural and
> life saving for your unique style.
> It is about honoring who you are
> inside, regardless of the tired
> stereotypes you have harbored
> for years, maybe decades,
> of who you should be.

Whatever your solutions are, first think about why you are packing your calendar so tight. The need to be indispensable, to be wanted, to be included is fairly basic, and stronger in some than others.[8] Saying no will not automatically reduce other people's regard for you, unless you do so rudely and without good explanation. *The underlying fear in saying no is that we won't be asked again.* Also, that we will somehow lose a relationship or other people's respect or affection by that word. To be brutally honest, there are some people for whom that is true. They like you more when you are pliable and agreeable. So, with eyes wide open, decide whether your peace of mind is worth the cost of this loss. I ask, therefore:

What would you do if you weren't afraid?

Chapter 4

Style Norms, Biases and Stereotyping

> During my technical education, we frequently used the term feedback. Literally, feedback is defined with respect to an attribute, with the purpose of adjusting to an optimal point.

I have always been different in some aspect. As a female student in an otherwise all-male classroom, gender stood out, but my *assertive style* fit right in. As an Asian, working for decades in North America, my focus on execution and speed that fit well with some cultures and organizations, was too direct in another.

Therefore, I am personally familiar with the biases and stereotypes associated with diversity. While race, religion and gender are more obvious and visual: style diversity is equally prone to bias and judgments. I am currently more outspoken than most; also a long-term thinker by instinct. Sometimes these differences work for me, at other times, they work strongly against me.

The two tools we will use in this chapter are:

- A self-assessment of your deep-rooted beliefs and norms around style.
- An original bias and stereotyping framework called The Five Judgments.

Together, these tools uncover values we hold strongly around good and bad personality traits, behaviors, overall style. *We all have style biases: the first step toward reducing them is understanding that they exist.* We tell people to speak up or stop talking so much; to be more assertive or less aggressive because "it doesn't look good on minorities, millennials, women (insert any stereotype here)."

Like master puppeteers we try to orchestrate behavior. If we have enough power, they comply and put on the desired mask. I understand this game exceedingly well. Wearing masks became so routine, sometimes it was hard to remember who the real person was inside. *We all wear masks, sometimes for our very survival. In the future my hope is that my mask be transparent, and rarely used.*

It can be a helpful self-exploration exercise to fill out this worksheet. And really think about unconscious messaging that has caused and reinforced, our values, beliefs, biases.

Author's Note: This tool is so important that it is in the body of the book, as well as in the appendix.

What Are My Style Norms and Biases?

Please circle or fill in the blank with the most accurate answer.

If you are uncomfortable documenting your responses, mentally answer the questions and process the learning internally.

- I would be _____ happy, embarrassed, relieved, OK either way (circle one or insert word here) if I were married to/dating a really chatty person.

  - This is because _____

    _____

    _____

- I _____ dislike/appreciate/admire/am curious about (circle one or insert word here) people who speak up for themselves, even if their viewpoint is controversial or against the majority opinion.

  - This is because: _____

    _____

    _____

- I feel _____ impressed by/uncomfortable around/ irritated by (circle one or insert word) people who are always well dressed and well groomed.

  - This is because: _____

    _____

    _____

- If I walked into a party with a large group of strangers and a few people I know, I would be _____ intimidated/exhilarated/neutral (circle one or insert word here)

  - This is because: _____

  _____

  _____

- I connect most with people who are _____ (age, culture, style, gender descriptor).

  - This is because: _____

  _____

  _____

- Being late for a lunch appointment with a close friend is _____not a big deal, rude, embarrassing (circle one or insert word)

  - This is because: _____

  _____

  _____

- I am annoyed by people who are/do/say _____ _____ (behavioral characteristic).

  - This is because: _____

  _____

  _____

Behavioral beliefs are learned in childhood or developed through personal experiences as an adult. They could be positive or negative traits about people around you.

Some of my behavioral beliefs about my peers and those around

me are: _____

_____

_____

_____

_____

The Five Judgments - A Style Stereotyping Framework

Overview:

This is an original tool I introduced in 2013 in my first book *Unleash the Power of Diversity*. There are judgments that people make about us, many of which have nothing to do with the caliber of our work or our output. These are often superficial judgments, made based on how we look, sound and behave: and they make or mar careers, relationships and lives.

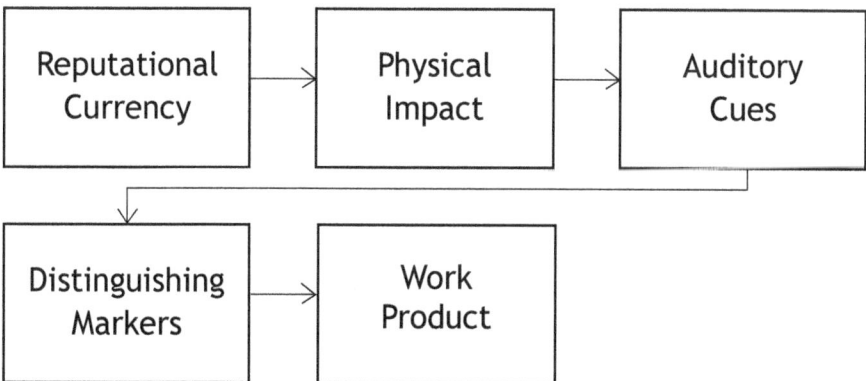

Figure 3: The Five Judgments - Source: Unleash the Power of Diversity

Reputational Currency: Long before you personally interact with a person at the office or workplace, she has preconceived notions of you. This could be based on your individual brand, word of mouth, or social media. If there is no data about you as a person, she will make a *judgment* of you based on her stereotyping and unconscious biases on this first element.

Physical Impact: As soon as you interact with this person, she forms *an impression* of you based on two key things: your visual appeal and the power you project. Visual appeal relates to attractiveness, clothing, posture, apparent age range, smell, fashion sense, and overall presence. In the style context, your body language, how you walk into a room, how you shake someone's hand and eye contact form critical first impressions of your personality.

Auditory Cues: The third element is based upon how you sound. This is a composite of pitch and tone of voice, giggles versus laughter, as well as the volume, speed, and number of words used. Unconsciously held beliefs cause us to judge the same thing differently depending on our frame of reference: for example, if a person speaks loudly, we may judge them to be confident, or too aggressive, depending on our point of reference.

Distinguishing Markers: A distinguishing marker refers to the three to five things that make you unique and different. *A distinguishing marker can be physical, behavioral or situational; what makes you stand out in one situation may be the norm in another.* This judgment is particularly critical in leveraging style diversity, as we uncover deep rooted biases toward or against specific traits.

Work Product: The fifth element relates to output: quality, originality, value, volume. Are you very good at your functional area of expertise? It is hard to accurately gauge output in most cases. So we measure it using proxies such as the person's vocal beliefs (or lack of) in their output...or how attractive their presentation slides are. Also noteworthy is the fact that *four judgments may occur before we examine a person's output.*

How to Use The Five Judgments Tool:

First, think about how people judge you based on The Five Judgments. If we don't understand how powerful these biases are, the stereotypical judgments people make about us within a few seconds, we are living in a fool's paradise. Pay special attention to your distinguishing markers. Later in the book, we will do more data gathering around this judgment. Next, think about the style judgments you make about people, particularly those different from you. If they are reserved, and you are outgoing; mild, and you are assertive: *how do you respond to them, label them, value them?* Apply this in the context of work functions: do you expect finance professionals to pay greater attention to detail, and sales people to be more outgoing than computer support?

Are you an extravert or an introvert, a hammer or a brush? That could determine how much you interact with strangers, or the way you behave in large groups, or whether you highlight your own or others' achievements. All these behaviors will have a direct impact on what people think about you, and on how you think about yourself. Your unique style results in judgments that have a powerful effect on your success and well-being. This process works both ways. Based on your style norms and biases (as you filled them out), you in turn are constantly making judgments, often unconsciously, about others. Is your Distinguishing Marker a confirmation of your line of work, or completely different? If the latter, maybe you are in the wrong line of work, because it pays so much — a golden cage that you need to fly out of?

Of all the judgments, the Distinguishing Markers are the most critical. They could relate to one of the other four judgments, or stand alone. A Distinguishing Marker in one situation is not so in another. My gender was of no consequence in an all-girls convent school; and often the only descriptor when I was a female student in engineering school. Your Distinguishing Markers are critical in self-discovery. Take time to reflect on your Distinguishing Markers. What they are now, and what you want them to be improved to, while remaining authentic.

List 3-5 of your Distinguishing Markers:

_____

_____

_____

_____

Now explain the concept to a few close friends, peers or family members, emphasizing the importance of honesty. Instead of asking leading questions like "don't you think my distinguishing marker is an attention to detail" ask open ended questions, so you get their unbiased feedback.

Here are some questions you can start the dialogue with:

1. What are my Distinguishing Markers?
2. What do people notice about me when they first interact with me?
3. What am I known for?

Write down what *they* list as your Distinguishing Markers

_____

_____

_____

_____

_____

Foundational Concepts and Skill Building Summary:

Skill building starts with self-awareness and other aspects of Emotional Intelligence, coupled with a clarity of our own communication style. We have style biases around how people, or we ourselves, should behave. When uncovering personal values and norms of individual and interpersonal behavior, characteristics include volume (chatty or reserved), assertiveness (strong or pleasant), timeliness (prompt or late) and flexibility (spontaneous versus organized). In addition to the EQi2.0 Emotional Intelligence Tool (mhs.com), I recommend the Myers Briggs Type Instrument (MBTI) for Personality and the Thomas Kilmann Instrument for Conflict Styles TKI (both at cpp.com).

During my technical education, we frequently used the term feedback. Literally, feedback is defined with respect to an attribute, with the purpose of adjusting to an optimal point. The purpose of a gauge is to take temperature readings, for example, in an air conditioning system such as a thermostat. If it says the temperature is too cold, that data is used to turn it up a degree.

If your assessment says you are too cold, turn up your temperature a degree. If you are too fired up to think straight, turn your emotional temperature down. That, in the physical sciences, is the immediate value of feedback. *Logic fails when our egos get in the way of feedback, morphing into denial or sugar coating.* The thermostat doesn't shout back to the valve: "No, you're wrong! I am not 69 degrees! How dare you label me that way!"

Life is simple when we leave our egos at the door. These are snapshots in time, malleable, changeable, and ready for the next round. If you want to get better, then use feedback the way it was meant to be used, as a valuable data point for course correction.

Section Three:
Why Are We Miserably Successful?

In this section, we will analyze:

- What makes us miserable

- Key stressors

- Sources of anxiety and tension

"Everything that can be counted doesn't count. Everything that counts cannot be counted."

Anonymous

Chapter 5

What Makes Us Miserable?

The title *Miserably Successful No More* is a little dramatic, intentionally: to grab your attention and really make you think. So you will realize that, perhaps, you are unhappily trapped in the golden cage of your success. Or, feeling empty inside, are living a life of quiet desperation. The first step is to autopsy the term 'miserably successful' with the thoroughness of a forensic pathologist.

The very act of defining success may be the root cause of your unproductive behaviors. Did you assume that money equaled success; and then, acquiring it, feel unhappy and unfulfilled? As you go through the list, identify specific factors you relate to with nonjudgmental self-observation.

Reflect on the things that shaped you early in life, and how has that worked for you? Take examples from young adulthood as well, listing critical events that impacted you from this phase. What are your 'funny mirrors': your optical illusions about your physical presence and personality? Perhaps you had a dominating boss as a new, young employee, who told you that your questions were absurd. If so, did that change your behavior? Make you stop asking those difficult questions? Factors such as sibling order, socio-economic status, parental power and educational levels impact our world view. We are molded by events around us: for example, our primary adult figure during our first three years of life is critical in shaping our beliefs and values.

What Causes the M.I.S.E.R.Y.?

- Materialism (equating personal value with physical objects or status)
- Incongruence (between purpose, actions and words)
- Stress (the explosion fueled by business demands, personality, resilience)
- Emptiness (feeling hollow and unfulfilled inside)
- Relationships (general or with specific people)
- Yeti (the Abominable Snowman of negative self-talk)

Author's Note: These results are based on polls, feedback from session participants, personal observations and informal interviews conducted over three years.

The objective is to identify and reduce derailers at their source. We will fail many times before we can reach lasting change. Therefore, resilience and self-forgiveness are critical. Authoring a book called *Miserably Successful No More*, I lapsed multiple times; self-sabotaging the book launch. You are reading this book now: therefore, I overcame these challenges obviously, though it felt overwhelming and impossible.

M is for Materialism

Materialism and affluence are two entirely different concepts. My definition of materialism:

> **"Materialism isn't about owning nice things—**
> **Materialism is about nice things owning you."**

A colleague and friend defined it as "a sense of contentment or joy at the possessing or gaining of material things." A surprisingly positive definition. However, he added, the more he and his family acquire, the more of his mental space it occupies. Materialism leads to a lack of simplicity: the more we have, the more we covet. How many of the things you chase are things you need — or are they things others have, that suddenly appear more attractive?

People often assume, mistakenly, that in order to be less materialistic, one must live a monastic existence in a cave or mountain miles away from humanity. Materialism is nebulous. It's not about owning the latest car or beautiful home. It's about why you purchased it in the first place. It's about whether I, as a person, need that car to get to my destination, and the ease with which it drives. As opposed to the fact that a certain luxury brand is required for executives at this company, or a house below a certain number of rooms or square footage would signal to the world that I haven't arrived. Interesting concept, that: *arriving*. It implies that one is going toward a goal, which, once reached, invites a full stop; when the truth is, one never arrives in life. One just tries to get closer to authentic impact and well-being.

Author's Note: There is a distinct difference between affluence and materialism. Many of you, readers, choosing to read a book entitled *Miserably Successful No More* are just that...successful, as defined in financial or quality of life metrics. Liking nice things and being obsessed by possessing stuff are two entirely different concepts.

My purpose in writing this book is that you read with purpose.

Let's pause in our reading for a minute. Think about, in your gut, whether you are materialistic or not. Remember your self-serving bias will kick in. I have justified buying branded shoes because they are more comfortable than regular ones: but is that really true? Further, do I need so many shoes? You and I both know the answer to those uncomfortable questions.

Here are three simple steps to reduce the hold of materialism:

1. *Assess which of your nice things own you, and which are the nice things YOU own.* Keep the ones you own: trade, give, and sell the others.
2. *Examine (and this is more difficult) whose story or rule is playing in your mind when you assign a value to something.* Perhaps a master's degree (your father's voice saying "An MBA will give you a stamp and more income" even though you really don't want to pursue it). Or a specific painting, which you never really liked but bought anyway.
3. *Imagine you had a financial overhaul. What would you need to be comfortable?* Not to survive — you have worked too hard

for too long — but to live with enough and a little more. Use that to determine what else can be donated to simplify your life.

Pause for a moment to reflect on each factor. When you have gone through the entire M.I.S.E.R.Y. acronym, determine which one is the sharpest pain point for you.

Ask yourself about the size and cost of items you own: do you have a compulsive need to collect things? Is the value of these items critical, or relatively unimportant to you? If you are a pack rat, that is a different discussion, related to clutter and a disorganized state of mind. Separate out the two. If you self-categorized as overwhelmed by clutter, focus on the Surroundings — Stress Section, as mentioned in Chapter 6. If it's something deeper, question your compulsion to get a home or car beyond your means. Have you fallen into the 'keeping up with the Jones' syndrome? And if the answer is yes, whose values are you mimicking: what is the hole you are trying to fill with objects?

Author's Note: If you prefer structured worksheets, go to the appendix. There is a checklist to inventory possessions as well as analyze clutter.

The Story of Christmas Debt -
a Groundhog Day Phenomenon

It was a shocker to me, when I first moved to the US, to observe a colleague's debt patterns. We were both working in the agronomy department of the local university.

Every November, she would go into a buying frenzy, maxing out her credit cards, to buy expensive gifts for her family. Spending hundreds of dollars on gift bags, wrapping paper, bows, cards and thousands on the actual gifts.

Then, she would be in debt for the rest of the year. Paying absurdly high interest rates on her credit cards, she would somehow get free of debt by August. A month or two of normal bills...and then the vicious cycle would start again.

With a brain freshly imported, using an entirely different Asian culture and mindset, I asked her, naively: "Why don't you agree, with your family, to exchange cards one year, or just $10 gifts for the children in the family? It might save everyone a lot of hassle...and I am sure your family would be horrified if they knew that you can't really afford these gifts?"

She looked at me as if I had suddenly grown an extra pair of ears; completely shocked. I realized that she would never change the pattern, unless something drastic happened, like bankruptcy. She was trapped in a prison of false pretenses, a materialistic identity defined by objects.

Your case may not be this extreme. You may just need a slight tweak of your approach to things. Take your family to a beach vacation instead of buying another expensive artifact. Create memories that last a lifetime, or give a chunk to a foundation or scholarship for needy children or young adults.

Ultimately it comes down to these questions:

- How much money, time and resources do you have to spend?
- How do you spend them now?
- How would you be best served, if these resources were freed up to do more good?

I is for Incongruence

Incongruence occurs when there is a contradiction between two things which should be aligned. It can feel like dissonance, deep in one's soul. Some examples of incongruence are:

- Words ≠ Actions
- Words and Actions ≠ Values
- Stated Values ≠ Truth
- Value 1 Actions ≠ Value 2

And so on...

The cost of incongruence can be very high, resulting in one or more of these outcomes:

- A degradation of self-worth
- A toxin that seeps into your skin
- A reinforcement of the Impostor Syndrome, which can lead to a chronic fear of being 'found out for who one really is'

- A loss of peace and equanimity
- An increase in stress levels

Let me explain with a couple of real life situations.

Words ≠ Actions Real Life Example of Incongruence[9]

Michael was lying down in a hotel room at the end of a busy day, and he was suddenly struck by two questions.

First of all, which city was he in? Beijing or San Francisco? Second, what was he doing here?

That's right...he was going for another award. The Sales Leader of the Year that he had won twice before. Which came with a fabulous all-expense paid vacation, and prestige and respect. And yet...

He had a loving family, which included a small child. Was he leaving her childhood behind? Rushing from place to place, missing important rites of passage? Her prize distributions, school concerts, just being with his family?

His words stated that his family came first. His calendar and actions told a different story. Two years later, he took the first, nerve-racking step toward changing his lifestyle.

Today, he is a successful independent consultant, who is there for the important and critical events for his family; and his own professional and personal growth. He has discovered that he loves to teach. One day, perhaps, he will become a full-time professor.

In the meantime, his calendar and his words are aligned.

He is miserably successful no more.

Let's discuss each of these aspects in more detail.

- Words ≠ Actions
- Words and Actions ≠ Values
- Stated Values ≠ Truth
- Value 1 Actions ≠ Value 2

Words ≠ Actions or Words and Actions ≠ Values

Let's go back to the *Two Truths and a Lie* Framework. If you self-assessed as being a brush, chances are that you don't say exactly what you think. In an effort to be polite, you are living in a world of euphemisms and white lies. And over time, this is making you feel dishonest inside, which leads to feelings of guilt or shame.

I know these feelings well as a people pleaser in my teens and twenties. Currently I am more of a hammer than a brush. Two decades of practice have made me more honest; however, this is a lifelong journey.

For those of you wondering how to move from glossy lie to palatable truth, try this simple first step. *Practice internally what you want to say for a month*. Do nothing, just *become aware of what you would have said or done if you were guaranteed that there would be positive results from your honesty*. Do this for every interaction where you are conscious of a feeling of holding something back.

You may be surprised at how often you are smiling when you don't feel like it. Saying it's OK when something is bothering you is like a piece of food stuck between your teeth: uncomfortable, vaguely annoying. After a month of noticing the (often surprising!) number of times you don't say or do what you honestly feel, let's move into phase one actions. Apply this only in a few low risk, simple situations. Let me bring this principle to life using a real situation; names have been changed for confidentiality.

Scenario: Reducing incongruence between words and thoughts

You and your friend routinely have lunch together. Your friend is a charming, strong minded person with very clear opinions. For years, you have been eating at barbecue and meat heavy restaurants because your friend likes them. You don't like meat much, and particularly dislike barbecue.

One day, you decide to say, before going for lunch with your friend. "I don't really like barbecue. Can we go to another restaurant instead?" Your friend looks surprised and says "Sure. Let's do Chinese." You almost feel deflated. If this was so easy, why didn't you do this years ago?

In this example, it worked out surprisingly well; all of your attempts will not go so well. Expect some push back, and be self-aware. If you are a brush, you will immediately want to back down and apologize. If you decide to stop rocking the boat due to that uncomfortable feeling in the pit of your stomach: don't give up. Refer to your Emotional Intelligence Self-assessment. Look at the summary slide and see which aspects are in play.

For example, can you increase your self-awareness and assertiveness? And perhaps be less flexible? And continually ask yourself, why you feel the need to be so polite and fearful of other peoples' disapproval? Above all, don't give up as soon as you hit a barrier.

Author's Note: A coaching client said frankly she wasn't sure this was the right time for change. The more I highlighted issues with her current style, the more she second guessed herself: to the point of not being sure of anything. This was actually a good sign, since she had been *unconsciously incompetent* (reference: the Ladder of Competence[10], a popular behavioral framework) and had now moved into *conscious incompetence*. Hopefully she will have both the skill and the will to move into *conscious competence*, perhaps eventually achieving the highest level, i.e. *unconscious competence*.

Value Misalignment: Stated Values ≠ Truth or Value 1 Actions ≠ Value 2

Pull out your calendar. Look at your vision statement. Now see how your calendar looks. What jumps out at you? Are the five to ten hours a week you spend on TV, movies and playing video games accurately captured somewhere?

If learning is so important, why have you not scheduled your own personal development this year? If helping is critical, how many hours of volunteer activities have you clocked? Have you donated enough to the charity you believe in to help little underprivileged children?[11] Given until it hurts?

The answer is uncomfortable. The temptation is to move on. Don't do it, reader. Don't move on. Listen to that voice, that conscience that says you are living a life of incongruence. Don't judge yourself, change your actions. Make one small change and see the ripple effect.

First, donate something of yourself — time, effort, objects, money. Next, encourage others to do the same. Why have I included a link, with a suggestion for a charity in my niece's name, to help underprivileged youth?[12] To make it easy for readers to give generously. This is an example of a ripple effect. Paying it forward until one reaches a tipping point or gains momentum.

How might your ripple effect play out? In addition to your personal donations of time and resources, how will you try and leverage your professional access for helping that scared, hungry little child in your mind's eye?

- What are the incongruences in your calendar, planner, daily routine?
- Why do they continue?
- What do you get from this habit or incongruence?
- What positive habit will you add as you remove the time drain?

Nature abhors a vacuum and rushes in to fill it. For example, people who stop smoking often resort to overeating. So when you stop doing something incongruent, make sure you quickly put in something of value.

Let's look at your last five critical interactions. How aligned were your words and actions? Did you have conflicting values? When values conflict, or if you are naturally more of a glossy brush, there is an excellent process that could help. It is called *Five Ways to Say Yes.*[13]

Interestingly enough, this is also useful in implementing your stop doing list.

Let's take an example. You are really busy at work. Your boss approaches you and asks you to actively volunteer (perhaps be a co-lead) for the United Way campaign at work. You like to help because it is a worthy cause. And...you are behind on three deadlines, one of them from that very same boss!

What are Five Ways to Say YES in this situation?

1. Yes, I will be happy to spend a few hours a week on United Way and be the project co-lead.
2. Yes, I will attend the kickoff meeting and speak with the lead about the project and time involved.
3. Yes, I will email/call the project lead and find out about it.
4. Yes, I will participate in United Way starting next week (once I have met your deadline).
5. Yes, I am interested in United Way. Noticing that there are a couple of pending deadlines, I wonder which one you suggest we push out by a week?

Do you notice a subtle movement as we went from options 1 through 5? That the 'yes' options are a combination of agreement and push back? And yet the word 'no' doesn't ever come into the conversation. Be as authentic as possible. Remember that you want to fulfill the need or request, at the same time don't have to jump to the 'full service car wash' mode right away.

Chapter 6

S is for Stress

> A chronic worrier has the
> psychological equivalent of tinnitus.
> The noise never really goes away.

After outlining the M.I.S.E.R.Y. acronym, we covered both Materialism and Incongruence in chapter 5; we will look at Emptiness, Relationships and Yeti in chapter 7. **Stress**, however, was so important, and evoked so much energy, inputs, and eye opening insights, that it needed one complete chapter. This chapter will outline the key causes of stress, and explore solutions to key stressors. Stress is key to reducing the 'miserably successful syndrome.' While the miserably successful among us may not experience several of the other factors: stress is the great equalizer. It is experienced by people across cultures, socio-economic status, gender, generations and style.

Why is this awareness pivotal in a book dedicated to diversity of style? Because we make ourselves miserable and cause self-imposed stress trying to fit into others' personality expectations first. Then, failing to understand how our family, friends, and colleagues are different from us, we cause *them* stress also. In informal interviews with audiences, session participants, readers, colleagues, as well as personal observations, the following stressor themes emerged.

Major Sources of Stress

- Time and Schedules (overload, deadlines, being late – most common)
- Internal Tendency (chronic nature: *"what if"* and *"did I"* worrying)
- Physical Appearance (weight listed most by women, otherwise for men)
- Relationships (typically one or two specific people, loneliness, divorce)
- Ego (unhealthy competitiveness, always having to be the smart one)
- Health (separately listed from weight, though of course correlated)
- Finances (not having enough money for survival)
- Loss (of youth, beauty, relationships, loved one. Fear of death and dying.)
- Violation of values (integrity and kindness were the most often listed)
- Work (mismatch with one's passion or skills, fear of being fired, boss)
- Politics (particularly in the U.S., in an election year)
- Performance (output quality, public speaking, tough interactions)
- Outliers (being different from mainstream, not fitting in)

There were a few others, also noteworthy: several of the stressors were interrelated. A person whose job was very stressful, with multiple deadlines felt it even more because of his natural tendency to worry. Some of these respondents set two or three alarm clocks before an important meeting... and still jumped up in panic through the night. Here's an acronym that summarizes the most major and frequent sources of S.T.R.E.S.S.

- Style (innate worrier - common topics: death, divorce, public speaking, items listed below)
- Time (work overload, schedules, family tension, being late, deadlines)
- Rx (health, both physical and emotional)
- Ego (the unhealthy need to win, trying to appear smart all the time)
- Substance (finances, even when person was wealthy, career/work content)
- Surroundings (home, office, car, cluttered things)

S.T.R.E.S.S. Issue Description and Costs to Health and Well-being

Style - An Internal Tendency to Worry:

This manifests itself as a chronic anxiety, a natural bent toward worrying. About oneself and others or, the world in general. Even in what should be the most enjoyable and rewarding of times, one cannot truly enjoy the moment because that inner voice is asking "Did I remember to lock the door/turn off the iron?" or "I wonder if my boss is upset with me" or "Is this milk past its expiration date?" or... Interestingly enough, things that were common stressors for some did not bother chronic worriers at all: the key is to become an expert at diagnosing your own.

The worry could be about the past (as listed earlier) or the future — 'what if' thinking. The constant fear of bad things about to land on one was crippling for people in this group. People spend a *huge* amount of energy worrying about outcomes they have completely no control over.

In a book devoted to style diversity, please understand that we are not pointing fingers here. I have always been a chronic worrier. Perhaps it started so young because I was around someone like that in early childhood. Or it was part of my inherent nature?

What are the things, (this is addressed to readers who are chronic worriers) that you worry about *all the time?* Ask yourself the following questions:

- Are they within your control?
- Are they worth the life-draining costs to your health and happiness?
- Are you slowly killing yourself through the thickening of your arteries, increasing your risk of a heart attack, your blood pressure?
- Are you changing the outcomes by worrying?

As they say, hope for the best and plan for the worst. Having contingency plans is different; specifically, assess the energy you waste worrying about the trivial or uncontrollable.

Let's address the last, pivotal, question listed above in more detail. In *Bridge of Spies*[14], the American attorney asks the alleged Russian spy facing a possible death sentence why or how he can appear so calm and unmoved. To which Abel (the alleged spy) replies "Will it help?" *That, in a nutshell is my advice for us, since this is a lifelong struggle for me as well.*

When you wake up in the middle of the night worrying, when you wake up tense, when you have anxiety in every pore of your being, can you ask yourself: "Will it help?"

Let me repeat myself, intentionally — something I rarely do — because this is so critical to chronic stress management.

"Will it help?"

If you can take action about it, do so. Life isn't always fair: things you wish didn't happen, can and will happen, and we have to deal with them. But, looking at the chronic worrying, following you like a shadow: ask yourself, as you feel it begin: *"Will it help?"*

Time: Schedules, Deadlines, Too Much to Do

In an increasingly frenetic world, this was a big one. Working too hard, there appeared to be an unreasonable demand on a person's time. Deadlines are always looming; we fear that many will be missed. There is just too little time. I know this feeling well and describe it as "always having a clock ticking in one's head, the constant feeling of rushing, of being late for something important."

This is another area where you must ask yourself, *how much of your time related stress is self-imposed?* This book has, ironically, caused me huge stress for two years. Setting an unreasonably high completion deadline, when health issues surfaced I imposed more stress on myself. In reality, no one was waiting for, or expecting, this second book. It would have been so enjoyable, after the first book was released, to simply savor the thrill of a new experience. Instead, there was a constant inner voice reminding me that I had failed by missing an aggressive, self-imposed publishing deadline.

So my first question to you is, how much of your deadline related stress was self-imposed? The second question is, how much of your calendar is within your control? The ability to say no, or stop doing things, is key. Also, we will go deeper into the *Five Ways to Say Yes* tool.

Rx: Health

Three aspects of health were major stressors

- Physical Health
- Chronic Pain
- Emotional Health

Physical health involved unhappiness with current weight, shape, appearance, especially where it stopped people from doing things they could do earlier. Some people were unfortunate enough to live with chronic pain and this impacted their entire quality of life. In rare cases, people had been diagnosed with life-threatening illnesses: this naturally consumed their waking thoughts and energy.

The final factor was emotional health, which has some alarming statistics associated with it. At a recent TEDx talk, Stephen Ilardi[15] referenced the growing rate of depression in the United States. Among thousands of aborigines, only a dozen or so were diagnosed with depression. While the percentage is fairly low for Americans currently in their sixties (around 5%); *for people under 25, this number is 25%; projected to be as high as 50% over time.* Please internalize this finding: that one out of two people, currently in their 20s, is projected to experience depression later on in life. A huge cause of depression for our younger generations has to do with bullying, a lack of tolerance and emotional safety.

> **Perhaps my view is jaded, but I believe that the best gift we can give our children is experience in losing, in failure.**

Ego: The Unhealthy Need to Win

Where physical appearance was skewed toward females, an obsessive desire to win was skewed toward the men in this survey.[16] People who experienced this phenomenon confessed to cheating if they felt they might lose. Even if the stakes were absurdly low, such as a game of bridge or family game night. Often, their identity was linked to being smart or winning, to the point of feeling threatened or at risk if they weren't always ahead.

Parents, thinking they are raising their child's self-confidence, often mistakenly turn their children into misfits. Constantly seeking instant gratification; getting prizes and rewards for breathing, in my opinion. *Perhaps my view is jaded, but I believe that the best gift we can give our children is experience in losing, in failure.* So they can learn how to do so gracefully. Self-confidence and ego are not to be confused with each other.

Ego becomes a stressor when our self-worth is linked to always being right, winning, or not losing face.

Substance: Money, Career, Content of Life Choices

The need for even more, a mismatch between their actual work content, career choice and skills or passion. Most of the people questioned were stable from society's perspective. Yet, many of them worried, some fiercely, about finances: there was a deep need, a hole that could not be filled enough. Fascinating. When I asked what number was enough to stop worrying, they quoted a figure.

My follow up question: "How much would that number have been five or ten years ago?" was eye-opening for many. *They currently possessed more than they had aspired to, crossing their financial stability goals.* Yet they continued to hold on to the fear and stress. Another stressor in the substance category was the actual work itself. For example, a person who was great in finance, and well rewarded, actually wanted to be an entertainer. So, there was a feeling of time rushing by, being trapped in a life of quiet desperation.

Surroundings: Home Office, Car, Clutter, People in that Space

This could include one's office, home, car, or not being on top of one's paperwork. People within this category were really stressed by their disorganized workspace or home. Some had post-it notes in stacks and piles all over their offices. Color coded. Another huge stressor was the inability to find things: keys, valuables, documents. Under stress, they tended to lose *more* things, *more* often, as their brains froze: prisoners of a vicious cycle. If this is one of your key stressors, the checklist in the appendix may help, as well as Marie Kondo's best-selling book *The Life-Changing Magic of Tidying Up*. Finally, and most interesting of all, surrounding's stress could be caused by *a person or persons being close by*.

After reading this list, look at your major stressors. You may have anything from just one to all of the factors listed. There is no right or wrong, obviously; what stresses you out stresses you out. Don't get bogged down by over generalization by age, gender, style, culture. Do men never worry about their weight? Are women never competitive? There are no absolute gender or other stereotypes in this discussion.

You now have a rough categorization of some of the key things that stress most of us. If you self-categorized as an innate worrier, wouldn't it be ironic if, by analyzing your stress, you added to it? Relax; at the very least, slow down your breathing and realize that recognizing an issue is a good first step in solving it. There are simple tools for all the factors.

Self-Analysis: Your Highest Sources of Stress:

As you analyze your top three S.T.R.E.S.S. factors, some things will jump out at you. Write them down. Take your time. Follow your first instincts. Then go back.

Which are the top three things in this list that cause you stress?

_____

_____

_____

Make a note of them in the blank space or circle the items listed earlier; we will revisit this at the end. Look at the multiple ideas and solutions to common stressors, customized to your style and personality.

Simple Stress Solutions

We will explore some solutions from research, personal observations and interview responses. These do not represent a complete set, they are designed to jog your memory, to a time when you, or someone you know, was able to successfully conquer stress. It goes without saying that the way you handle stress will be unique to your style. An introvert may find great peace in solitude. An extravert will relieve that same stress by talking it out with people, together or separately.

Solutions for Style: An Internal Tendency to Worry

Self-awareness and the recognition of being a chronic worrier is the first step. You cannot alleviate this issue if you don't acknowledge that it exists. Make a note, look at the words people use around you, above all, let your guard down and be open to feedback. A manager at work who knew me beyond the façade (remember, I fooled most people with a calm demeanor) would quietly say "Take a deep breath. It's going to be OK."

Let's unpack this more fully. The chronic worrier almost never fully enjoys a waking moment, is never at peace. In the middle of magnificent achievements, there are worries "did I lock the house ...car...leave the iron on...forget to mail that check?" At some point or the other, almost all of us have gone back home to check if we left the door unlocked or a stove on, or something similar. That is what one would call typical worrying. What the chronic worrier does is obsessively fret about something, anything, almost all the time. About whether their house is being burgled while they are on vacation, or whether their children will look after them in old age. This is a never-ending process: It's like being perennially tuned to a really bad radio station, where every second the message is blasting in your inner ear "Oh no! What if..."

There is an unusual physical condition, called tinnitus, literally, a ringing in the ear. In rare cases, this ringing is so loud and disruptive that it impacts the quality of that person's life, interfering with sleep patterns, relationships and success at work. *A chronic worrier has the psychological equivalent of tinnitus. The noise never really goes away.*

> **It is like being perennially tuned to a really bad radio station, where every second the message is blasting in your inner ear: "Oh no! What if..."**

Once you have become aware of this stressor, and accepted that you have this tendency, the next step is what I call *'positive what if'* thinking. *What is the worst* that can happen to you, *if* that thing you were afraid of happened? Take both practical and psychological steps to reduce worrisome situations. For example, if you are afraid that you left the iron on, invest in an iron that shuts itself off. If you are afraid of being laid off, talk to a financial advisor or analyze your finances yourself.

Surrounding yourself with calmer people versus chronic worriers is another great solution. Finally, there are many people who believe in the long-term effects of deep breathing and meditation techniques that can slow down the mind and reduce stress over time.

Some of you will recognize this description as applying to you immediately. I am so sorry that you have suffered so much for so long. Others will read the words, and understand it in your brains, but not quite get this phenomenon, which is good. You are most likely not a chronic worrier (or in severe denial). Does this apply to someone in your family, a friend, or a colleague? Please advise them to read this chapter.

Solutions for Time: Schedules, Deadlines, Too Much to Do

Time can involve work overload, or family-work tension, being late, not meeting deadlines, an over-packed schedule. During particularly stressful times, when these things tend to overwhelm us, the first step is recognizing danger zones. This is linked to our self-awareness aspect of Emotional Intelligence; e.g. *do not take it for granted that intense deadlines are stressors for everyone.*

Speaking with an air traffic controller (who has thousands of people's lives in her hands) you may assume that the person is highly stressed. And indeed, that person may be: or, she may be exhilarated by the complexity of the situation, and the heady feeling that she can conquer and solve it. Time and schedules need to be managed if they cause us stress.

Two solutions to deadline-related pressures are Calendaring (both strategic and tactical time management) and Root Cause Analysis.

1. **Calendaring:**

   Find a system that works. For most people, it's a combination of virtual (online calendars) and physical (planners, wall or desk calendars, boards).

A few fundamental principles:

1. If it's important put it on the calendar.
2. If it's on the calendar, ask if it's important.
3. Plan consistently for the day, week, month and year ahead.
4. Don't lie to yourself about how you spend your time.

Simple? Yes. Easy? No.

I am aware that, in a book on style diversity, we must acknowledge that people are polar opposites in time management. If having post-it notes all over your office and home are common for you, there is a good chance you are P in MBTI.[18] If you are a J in MBTI — a list maker, checking off calendar items, planning for the week — you will resonate with these ideas. Adapt these ideas to suit your style.

Look at your vision. Make sure that what Stephen M.R. Covey[19] called the Big Rocks (time with family, self-nurturing, career networking, doctor visits) are in your calendar first. Don't get caught in busywork while taking no steps toward your vision.

This is a process I want you to follow mindfully. *Process is as critical as content in behavior change.* This realization has been immensely powerful for me.

Let's harvest this data together. Look at the first item. When you put important things in your calendar, you are being strategic. You are also adding things which will take up time. So you must have an equal or greater item, to remove in that time period, for the math to work. It's simple and logical. The last item, remove stressors and time wasters is a tactical remove. This frees up time for the corresponding add. I share these tips with you because this list is just a starting point. Customize this process for yourself. Always keeping intact the logic of a 24-hour day, with hopefully an 8-hour sleep allowance built in. Be sure to categorize as 'Strategic' or 'Tactical' and as *Adding* or *Subtracting* from your calendar.

- Put the important things in your calendar first (Strategic - *Adds)*
- Analyze and change self-imposed deadlines and unrealistic expectations (Strategic)
  - o Reflect on why you set them in the first place
  - o Let your calendar reflect your new thinking
- Build in buffers for everything you possibly can[20] (Tactical – *Adds)*
- Watch out for high stress periods, build extra cushion (Tactical – *Adds)*
- Review your calendar weekly, monthly and annually and continuously improve calendaring (Strategic and Tactical – *Adds and Subtracts)*
- Remove or reduce time wasters, or worse, stressors[21] (Strategic and Tactical – *Subtracts)*

Hopefully by now you are seeing how multiple aspects of what makes you miserably successful can be managed, according to your unique and different style. And that they all overlap, are intertwined. Find what works for you. Let this start your juices flowing, so you can design what is of aid to *you*.

<u>**Author's Note**</u>: My final tip is, *adjust the buffer between meetings and events depending on the criticality of the event itself.* So if you like to be 10 minutes early, for a relatively low criticality event, leaving 10 minutes early is fine. However, add a multiplier if it's more important. I use 2X multiplier buffers for moderately important, and 3X multipliers for critical items (such as catching an international flight).

If you find this type of calendaring too prescriptive, it's good to know this about yourself. Take a couple of ideas from it and move on: calendaring is a tool. Your actions reflect your purpose. Do your actions say you are drifting meaninglessly through life; helplessly pulled along by a tide of 'shoulds'? Or, are you rowing with intent toward a destination? The first part of this book was about understanding your destination in life. This section is about making the time to reach that destination.

2. **Attacking the Root Cause of the "Too Much to Do" Syndrome:**

   a. Analyzing the syndrome using the *'Five Whys'* tool
   b. Learning the *'Five Ways to Say Yes'* technique (if the root cause is taking on too much)
   c. *Understanding the need* that is met by agreeing so much

The Five Whys[22] is a Quality Control tool also used in Statistical Process Control analyses. We will use it to examine why you got here in the first place.

1. Why are you so stressed because of time and schedules?

Let's say the answer is, you are too busy, have too much to do. Using 'The Five Whys' approach, we will dig deeper into the root causes of your behavior.

2. Why are you so busy?

Answer: There are two deadlines both coming up in the next three weeks and I have promised to host a huge retirement party. Also, my colleague retired and, until his replacement is found, I am doing double duty.

Take any one of these sub answers and ask a related question.

3. Why are you filling in for your retired colleague, given your already heavy work load?

Answer: Because my boss asked me to take on the extra work.

4. *<u>Why do you say yes to everything your boss asks you to do?</u>*

This fourth question is probably the most critical of the series, because it may be symptomatic of a trend versus a one-time event.

- Try to remember the last time you said no to this boss.
- Honestly compare your workload to that of your colleagues.
- Reflect on how your coworker, when asked the same kind of question, responded differently.
    - o She asked your boss which of her current projects could either be delegated to someone else, or delayed, in order to clear up some time for this new project.

Now, let's apply the data harvesting and pattern recognition process to this situation. Asking the final question:

5. Why are you afraid to say no to your boss?

There are no right or wrong answers to this question. Just the truth. The answer may be because of the boss' strong temperament (talks very loudly, very opinionated, sharp tongued)...or exactly the opposite. Quiet and soft spoken, you respect him so much that you don't ever want to say no and disappoint him. Because he has done so much for your career. There are clearly multiple possible responses to this question. Once we get closer to the root of the problem, we can ask:

What would you do if you weren't afraid?

This powerful question can open up new worlds of possibilities. If you were guaranteed there would be no negative consequences to speaking your mind. And if you were assured that the relationship with the other party would stay as good, or even become stronger, what would you say and do?

Solutions for Rx: Health

You already know what a healthy lifestyle means. You are just not spending time doing *what you know* to be good for you. If this is a big stressor, take a small step. Let's consider three aspects of health:

Physical Health - Maintaining and improving. Physical health involves basic things like eating well and adequate movement. You already are intelligent enough to know what's good for you, so let's not waste each other's time. If you know that walking 10,000 steps, or exercising moderately for 30 minutes 3 times a week will make you feel better, then why aren't you doing it? I am intentionally keeping this section really short. If you are serious about improving your physical well-being, start executing plans toward that goal. Schedule that overdue doctor's visit, sign up for a gym or walking program, go out to buy healthy foods that you like.

Chronic Pain - Alleviation. A few of you are unfortunately dealing with chronic pain. Those of you who are not in chronic pain, take a minute to imagine a world where you are suffering every waking moment of your life. I hope this realization makes you take some steps (couldn't resist the pun!) right now.

Health Issues - Serious, possibly life threatening. If you have been diagnosed with a potentially fatal or life threatening illness or condition, first of all, I am so sorry. If you cannot improve your health at this time, make things right where possible with closure, and pass on your message. Let that be your legacy. There are so many examples of brave people who have done exactly that: the Steve Jobs video on his deathbed, the inspirational video of Randy Pausch (*The Last Lecture*).[23] I highly recommend that you see the latter: an intelligent, successful man deciding what to do with the last few weeks of his life, following a fatal diagnosis of pancreatic cancer.

Instead of slowly dying a quiet, sad death, Dr. Pausch spoke at multiple venues for as long as he could. He delivered an absolutely inspirational speech about how to deal with negative feedback, how to apologize, value people over things, show gratitude, how to dream.

Take the time to decide what your legacy is. Just months before dying of pancreatic cancer in 2007, Dr. Pausch said: "If you live your life the right way, your dreams will come to you. I choose to have fun today." His question: "Are you a Tigger or an Eeyore?" referred to the choice we have, which impacts both our physical and emotional health, of complaining versus working harder while having fun. And when the end comes, as it will one day for all of us, which kind of legacy would we like to leave? That of a Dr. Randy Pausch, who was truly inspirational — or — nothing?

So What Is the Solution to Emotional Health Issues?

Obviously, I have no background in any of these areas, so consult with a professional if you are experiencing emotional health issues and please follow their clinical and expert advice and diagnosis. That in fact, is my first suggestion: to take this seriously and address the issue. Too many lives have been lost in ignoring this topic because of the social stigma around it. Also, there are several cultures where this is considered to be a made-up issue, so breaking that cultural stereotype is critical. Finally, a word on bullying. Why do we, as parents, let our kids get away with being bullies? Conversely, why do we allow our children to be bullied without equipping them with coping and resilience skills?

We need to take responsibility for the way we treat others and how outside influences affect our personal emotional health. *Just as we should not tolerate bullying behavior in others, so also should we be keenly aware of the impact of our own actions.* Do we understand the very real difficulties associated with specific emotional health issues? Getting to the bottom of these issues, with professional guidance, can help alleviate stress in other areas.

I believe firmly in the power of massage, breathing, meditation and nontraditional remedies to multiple health issues. Particularly stress related. Also, if we have successfully navigated through the stop doing chapters, and taken out hours of couch potato television viewing and video games, we are already ahead of the health game.

Normal, preventative health is a matter of habit: breaking the bad ones and replacing them with healthy ones. Listen to your body and mind: what do they crave? Silence? Then turn off the noise. And so on.

Solutions for Ego: The Unhealthy Need to Win

This can be linked to a destructively competitive nature, having to appear the smartest person in the room.

How does one know that one has proceeded to the unhealthy competition versus constructive competition?

Miserably successful people, in my experience, have more than a representative share of cut throat competitiveness, of leaving body bags, of winning at all costs, often resulting in short term gains. The inner cost of this unhealthy competitiveness is twofold. First of all, the toll it takes on the body and health. Linked to Type A personalities (all Type A's are not unhealthy competitors, obviously), there have been studies linking physical stressors to health. Can, and does, this characteristic cause thickened arteries and increase your risk of strokes or heart ailments?

Second, the cost to interpersonal relationships. Does this person want to win at all costs? Is he, therefore, a sore loser? Is this person's identity inextricably dependent on being seen as the smartest, strongest, best person in the room? In other words, is he miserable if he loses, regardless of how low the stakes are? How can a healthy relationship thrive under these circumstances?

Recognize the pattern, even if you do not have this trait. The key is not always the content (win or loss), but the process of arriving at it. Get honest feedback from someone who will give you the palatable truth; if you are not yet ready for the hammer. If you can take it, the hammer is the one which can change your behavior. The feedback I received, decades ago, about dysfunctional competitiveness was so shocking that maintaining the status quo was no longer an option.

Solutions for Substance: Money, Career, Content of Life Choices

If you are reading a book called *Miserably Successful No More* there is a high probability that you are financially comfortable, perhaps even wealthy. And yet...many of you worry about not having enough. We introduced the idea of never having enough in M is for Materialism. This section relates to the stress that is caused by finances and substance. However, there are three questions that will help you deal with this stressor:

1. How much do I need?
2. How much do I have?
3. Will I feel financial stress no matter how much money I have?

The third question is particularly critical to self-awareness. If the honest answer to the third question is yes, then this worry around substance has nothing to do with the substance itself. Go back to the Emotional Intelligence and self-awareness chart on page 37 and reflect on which aspects trigger your worries. Low self-regard, optimism or stress tolerance?

Author's Note: Obviously, if finances are a stressor because of insufficient funds, the solution set is different, and beyond the scope of this book. Please consult a financial professional for ways to reduce outflow, and increase intake.

Solutions for Surroundings: Home Office, Car, Clutter, People in that Space

> Reflect on the *need that 'holding on to stuff' is fulfilling*. How can you meet that need without holding on to the thing itself?

If clutter and disarray is a source of significant stress in your life, read Marie Kondo's New York Times Bestseller *The Life-Changing Magic of Tidying Up*. It has changed many lives. While implementing the MarKon system may feel like a big undertaking, it can be a game changer if you practice her techniques successfully. If this is a top stressor, be open to her ideas without getting overwhelmed. Don't go for perfect. Reflect on the *need that holding on to stuff is fulfilling*. How can you meet that need without holding on to the thing itself?

For example, if you have a sentimental attachment to your child's small clothes, keep a favorite sweater if it means that much to you. Then take pictures of everything else. Imagine that underprivileged child who will be warm because of these clothes. Then put everything in bags and give it away before you have time to start taking things out. Lingering is the enemy of uncluttering.

Now would also be a good time to go back to the M is for Materialism checklist in the Appendix, and see what jumps out at you. This will help prioritize the uncluttering. Examine what makes you hold on to, or acquire, so many things that it is cluttering up your physical and emotional space.

We have seen a lot of stressors and explored many ideas for reducing the critical ones. Before we get overwhelmed, or move on to the next chapter, let's take stock and make some concrete commitments to change.

Summary: Reducing Stress Worksheet

List your top three stressors.

_____

_____

_____

If you had the answer, what would it be?

_____

_____

_____

_____

What is one thing you will do to reduce the worst of your stressors, from this moment onward?

_____

_____

_____

_____

At this point, reader, you may become a little overwhelmed and decide all this is too much work.

That's okay. Very typical, in fact. Don't stop, or give up, or give in. Just pick one thing. Do it in chunks. Get the help of your support systems. Then find the time to do something about it. It is that logical and simple.

Four powerful questions to help conquer stress:
1. *Is reducing stress important to you?*
2. *What is the cost of doing nothing?*
3. *What could you do if you weren't afraid?*
4. *What are you waiting for?*

Chapter 7

Completing the M.I.S.E.R.Y. Analysis

E is for Empty

Empty has many faces. The first one has names like Impostor Syndrome: hollow and shell-like. It's the feeling that life, or, specifically, my life, has little purpose or relevance.

The phenomenon of emptiness is extremely dangerous. It can lead to toxic behaviors, and in the extreme, even thoughts of self-harm. Accompanied by depression, feelings of helplessness, fatigue and loneliness. Friends and family members, know that you can literally save lives by recognizing the warning signs of this phenomenon. If you are experiencing this, the best advice I can offer is to reach out. You may be feeling terribly alone in addition to the burden of emptiness. Sharing these difficult feelings can significantly lessen the distress.

Let's examine where you fall in the frantic and frenetic scale.

- Do you try to fill every waking moment of your life with other people, endless hours of mind-numbing television, other mindless activities?

- Is every day a whirlwind of events?
- When was the last time you sat, and quietly reflected, instead of working off a long 'to do' list?

> **Don't be afraid of quiet time.**
> *You are worth spending time with,*
> *alone and free from distractions.*

When we constantly overfill our time and lives like this, it begs the question: What are we running away from? What are we afraid to face in the silence of our own thoughts? If you find yourself, reader, squirming uncomfortably and not wanting to read any further, that is good. No, that is *excellent* because that signals a first step toward removing your protective layers and masks.

There is a discomfort associated with lasting change: are you willing to lean into it? The unwrapping of the empty phenomenon lies in slowing down and allowing ourselves to **stop** doing things. Some of these traps are social niceties or obligatory time-wasting activities that you don't enjoy, with people that you don't like, linked to you by birth or circumstances. Don't be afraid of quiet time. *You are worth spending time with, alone and free from distraction*. This may be a novel concept, but it is very powerful. Deep inner peace can come from it. Different from meditation, what I am suggesting is that you exercise curiosity and get to know yourself better.

"What a strange and alien concept. I know myself already," you may be thinking. Possibly true: however, if I ask *'What else might be true?'* let me propose an alternative. Have you, perhaps, in trying to learn about everyone else around you never really asked yourself *"Who or what am I?"* What would happen if you got to know and appreciate yourself (if you don't already)? Do you believe in Cato the Elder's[24] quote: 'I am never less alone than when alone'?[25]

> The key is to assess the ratio of internal-to-external interactions that works best for you. Learning how to balance stillness and sound, find the combination that results in your most productive self.

Of course, in a book about style diversity, we must acknowledge preferences based on our personalities. Extraverts may prefer to talk about a topic versus quietly thinking about it. I have a love-hate relationship with sounds, socializing and external stimuli. After a wonderful and inspiring family reunion, the cool silence of my writing 'cave' is pure bliss. After a week of solitary silence, punctuated only by the soothing hum of the air conditioner, I am ready to re-enter a sound filled human world. The key is to assess the ratio of internal-to-external interactions that works best for you. Learning how to balance stillness and sound, find the combination that results in your most productive self.

To summarize:

- Assess how empty you feel inside.
- Next, examine whether you are trying to mask emptiness

with a flurry of activity.

    o   Don't judge yourself. Make conclusions based on data, how you spend your time, who you spend it with, how often you are alone.

- Third, go deeper into self-discovery, to learn who you are and what fills you physically and mentally.

What do we do when we are constantly in a state of emptiness? Watching a movie with my mother last night, a verse in a song struck me, loosely translated: "I have swum in the seven seas, but my soul is thirsty and dry." An easy way to reduce your emptiness is to fill another's life, donating either money or time. Sitting in a plane next to a remarkable veteran, I was intrigued by his life lesson: "Give until it hurts." Challenging him, I asked whether he lived this mantra. He looked quizzically at me and said: "You be the judge. I served in my country's wars and lost most of my hearing. When my mother-in-law developed Alzheimer's, I left a lucrative job and moved across three states so my wife could be there for her. And now, a grandfather, my son's and daughter's families live with us, because they can't afford to live on their own, due to medical and financial reasons."

"Yes," I replied, in deep admiration. "You *do* give until it hurts."

Author's Note: When trying to gauge whether your life is empty or not, you may get defensive, which is perfectly natural: be aware of this and proceed anyway.

We often experience a strong, even frantic, urge to fill a void. Alcohol, food, drugs, gambling, sex, nicotine, entertainment (television, music, concerts, movies) chatter and forced togetherness are some of our desperate crutches. Many of these things aren't destructive, per se. There is nothing wrong with food, obviously —we wouldn't survive without it. However, after attending a Mindful Eating workshop, conducted by the amazing Dr. Jan Chozen Bays[26], I realized that many of us fill our mouths because our souls are empty.

Empty can be cured — empty has a non-compulsive solution. And, conversely, empty will never be solved if we deny, to ourselves, that the compulsion exists. If we spend hours gambling, simultaneously on two slot machines, we may be trying to fill a void inside. What is the purpose of hitting buttons so mechanically that we do not notice how much money we have won or lost? For three years, I observed multiple aspects of these behaviors. Let's look at the whole pull of Las Vegas. *'Too much'* was my first impression: lights *too bright*, sounds *too loud*, costumes *too flamboyant*. There was a man-made nature to the entire area: in stark contrast to the majestic Grand Canyon not too far away.

To clarify, as with most coins, there are two sides: Las Vegas also happens to be a popular vacation choice for our family. The shows are amazing, there are fabulous things to do. Further, one can experience astounding uses of technology as in the magnificent and realistic 'sky' inside Caesars Palace. Free shows abound: choreographed fountains at Bellagio, volcanoes erupting in Mirage, light shows on Fremont Street. All making it worth the visit. So it's not the condemning of a city. More an observation of the sadness and emptiness of compulsive escapism. This may take the form of obsessive gambling, or other vices freely available, no questions asked, in places like this. A very different mindset, obviously, from a group of friends placing a few bets before grabbing dinner and a show.

I personally observed a young man, in a red T-Shirt, standing in front of a high limits slot machine late one night. The next morning, after checking out of the hotel, we walked past that same area. There was Mister Red T-shirt, still hitting the same machine, at the same frenetic pace. The T-shirt now crumpled, the eyes reddened and blank. Almost as if he was afraid to get back to the silence of his hotel room, to be alone with his thoughts and company. Of course, this is an extreme case.

Think of five examples of empty that come to mind as you read this section. Yours or others. Do away with the judgments. Just think about the actual facts of these five situations. What was the vehicle for escape? Did the addiction get stronger and stronger? How does this story end...or is it ongoing? Reflect on what you have learned from these examples, before reading on. *Do you feel, or have you ever felt, empty inside?* Most of us do, at some point in time. And if the answer is yes, how often do you experience this feeling? Be honest. How do you cope with it: do you dive into (a bottle of, plate of, hand of, the arms of) something that makes you forget? Do your actions, choices, companions make you better, or do they help you forget reality?

Our alumni group does volunteer math tutoring for underprivileged children because we were blessed with good technical education. And, the surprising outcome is, we benefit more from the sessions than the children we tutor. There's no shame in suffering the empty syndrome. There is a global epidemic of lonely people. The solution to empty, of course, depends on your nature. If you find it hard to reach out to others, then confessing to feeling empty may appear shameful to you.

It is through kindness, to ourselves and others, that we fill this void. And this kindness may need huge courage, to recognize our or others' loneliness. We can try to fill that void in a healthy manner. Good with your hands? Join a Habitat for Humanity work group, and build a house with someone. Very hard to work alongside someone for a good cause for weeks and not build up any kind of connection.

Author's Note: Share this moment with me: the sun's dappled rays slipping through ivory blinds; the only sound a laptop's hum. Writing these words, I visualize you reading them, and in your stillness and solitude, regaining your equilibrium, your inner comfort. So, the two of us, while completely apart in reality, are as one: aligned in the peace of this quiet, powerful moment.

R is for Relationships (General Conflict or One or Two Triggering People)

Some people have a hard time making, and keeping relationships. If that describes you, pay special attention to the section in Chapter 2 on Emotional Intelligence. Focus on interpersonal relationships, and how you can make them mutually satisfying. Also, examine your self-awareness (usually low in people with chronic relationship issues), assertiveness (extremes are both danger factors, too high can be unpleasantly aggressive, too low may cause people to disrespect you). To summarize:

1. Rebuild your most important relationship first - with yourself.
2. Analyze the five most critical relationships in your life.
   a. Take action on the most stressful one.
   b. Take time to be grateful about the easy ones.

Rebuild your most important relationship first – with your self

I am continually surprised by a very obvious (to me) anomaly when it comes to relationships. We disregard the most important and lasting relationship of all, in order to gain approval in the eyes of others, some of whom are even strangers. We ask ourselves: "What would so and so do? What would make that person happy? How can I help this other person?" without offering the same courtesy to ourselves.

"What is my relationship with myself?" is a critical, non-trivial question.

Am I comfortable in my own skin?

Do I blindly accept advice from all and sundry, or does self-regard allow me to ignore inaccurate criticism?

Am I pleased with my achievements?

Do I applaud myself for having worked so hard, not just for the necessities of life, but also for the comfort and independence I have earned?

If I am not at ease with myself, this bleeds into my relationships with others. We teach people how to relate to us, how to, or not to, respect us, whether we are worthy of that promotion, that opinion, that shoulder to cry on. If you are not inflicting stress on yourself, that is excellent. You can now move on to analyze how you allow others to get under your skin.

Analyze the most critical relationships in your life

    a. Take action on the most stressful one.

    b. Take time to be grateful about the easy ones.

Relationships, in general, can be stressors for some people. This could be because they have a superiority complex, or are low in Emotional Intelligence, or are highly demanding. This could be because (this sounds shallow, and is, unfortunately, true) they are not charismatic enough for people to tolerate their imperfections.

How will you gauge your competence in building and sustaining relationships? Think back to the last ten negative interactions you had. Were they all with one person or with different people? *If you have tension involving multiple people, this could be an indicator that you are the common thread.* If you can easily come up with several examples of unpleasant interpersonal interactions within the last year— that is a data point. Don't get defensive. Look at both your Emotional Intelligence numbers as well as your conflict resolution style.

There are two completely different sets of strategies for this section, depending on what the pattern is. The first question is, which are your most important relationships? Regardless of whether we are single or married, parents or siblings, there are some people that are precious to us: friends or family. We don't get to choose where we are born, but we do get to choose on whom we spend our time and energy.

While our family can be, and often is, our main go-to for close relationships, it can also cause us the most pain. Knowing all the skeletons in their closets, some relatives or friends are callous enough to use this information as a weapon. Using self-awareness and Emotional Intelligence, list your top five relationships. Label them as high or low in terms of stress, rewards, maintenance, and triggering of emotions.

1. Person A:
    a. Most important person in your life (high reward, low stress).
    b. Very easy to be around, unassuming, selfless, kind (low maintenance).
    c. Being in conflict with this person is painful, this happens rarely (medium negative emotions).

    Decision: Obviously a keeper, huge positives, low cause of stress, no brainer.

2. Person B:
    a. Your boss (high stress by nature of the relationship).
    b. Very high expectations, tough, abrasive (high maintenance).
    c. He holds a grudge against his enemies. At the same time, he does provide you visibility with senior leaders (mix of high risk which is negative, and sponsorship which is positive).

    Decision: Complex. How many choices do you have? Most likely you will need to be in this relationship because of your boss' situational power. What you can choose to do is build a buffer, a layer of 'virtual bubble wrap' to protect your equanimity and health.

3. Person C:

    a. An aging parent (high concern over their health, an amazing source of strength your entire life- mixed adder and remover of stress).
    b. Pure joy to spend time with (low maintenance).
    c. Worried about their physical safety as they get older. Conflict with other family members around this issue (Mixed: mostly positive).

Decision: Complex. There is no leave or stay choice here. It is a given that you will be in this relationship for the duration. No question. What you can choose to do is make practical decisions, flex and always keep the positives in front. Manage this by giving good advice and ensuring the most practical help as time goes by, either outsourced or in person. Reduce the squabbles with family members over this. Always keep the end in mind: your common goal is your parents' well-being.

You get the idea.

List your top five relationships and see which are fine as is and which need adjustment.

Person A_____

Person B_____

Person C_____

Person D_____

Person E_____

Identify the one/s that need adjustment.

Congratulate yourself on the important relationships in your life that are fulfilling and relatively low in stress. What a blessing if those happen to be with your family, boss, friends. Now look at the thorns in your side, the people that cause you to toss and turn at night: do the low-hanging fruit first. If there is a venomous relationship (not necessarily a venomous person, but the interpersonal dynamic is toxic) that is not critical to your survival, drop it. To clarify, this is with someone other than your top five. We are practicing our skills by eliminating a minor relationship first, before moving up to major, high impact ones.

Do it and don't look back. I have personally done this twice in my life: it was surprisingly easy. Virtually no guilt (except during the actual conversation or while blocking the first few calls and emails); just satisfaction that I had the guts to take action and walk away. You are stronger than you think. This is a low risk drop, remember. You are not leaving your job or storming up to your boss or removing yourself from the life of your partner or parent without thought or calculation. Use the common sense that is increasingly uncommon to make your first practice selection.

Now let's take it up a notch and look at the most critical relationships in our lives. A colleague described this (in another context) as "Who are the people at home or work, without whom life stops? And, conversely, whose life stops without you?" If 'stops' is an extreme word for your practical nature, replace it with 'becomes difficult,' or 'is hard to function.' You are trying to manage your relationships to protect your well-being or reduce stress: permanently or at this juncture in your life.

Analyze your relationships first and list options such as:

- Leave the relationship.
- Redefine the relationship.
- Reduce the stress while staying physically in the situation.

What are the potential benefits of taking these actions? Equally important, what is the costs of *inaction* to your health, inner self, stress level? There are often elements of choice in relationships. I close with a quote found by my insightful and talented nephew RG: "Truth is; everybody is going to hurt you; you just have to find the ones that are worth suffering for."

If this sounds too cynical for an optimist, read it again. If you still have a strong visceral, opposing reaction to this, reverse the subject of the quote. What if you are the cause, not the receiver — have *you never hurt every single person* that you care about? The keepers are the ones who can see past the hurt to the value of compromise, forgiveness and beyond.

The CEO's Umbrella

One of my favorite clients is the CEO of an established Fortune company. Let's call him Tom. I have met with Tom fairly regularly for several years, individually and with his executive team.

One afternoon, it was raining torrentially, as it does sometimes in Texas. Trying not to get my hair wet, I pulled out my umbrella (a thoughtful gift from someone else) and dashed into Tom's corporate offices.

Just outside his office, Tom's assistant Pat rushed forward to help me. She quietly took the umbrella out of my hands, and put it away behind her in a corner to dry.

I walked into Tom's office, trying not to splatter too much water onto his lovely mahogany table.

An hour later, the rain had abated, and I walked out of Tom's office. Pat kindly handed me my umbrella, neatly folded, and I tucked it under my arm. It felt a little heavy, but I was so engaged processing the output from the meeting that I didn't notice.

Driving home, I was surprised to receive a call from Pat.

In it, she said apologetically "Debjani, unfortunately I gave you Tom's umbrella by mistake. He flies out to Connecticut this afternoon, so I gave him your umbrella to use."

I immediately jumped into Yeti (the abominable snowman of negative self-talk) mode. First of all, how could I have been so careless as not to notice how heavy and beautiful the Davek umbrella was?

Oh no, what would Tom think about my umbrella...it had been part of a welcome gift bag. I had no idea how sturdy it was, it was definitely not a brand name like his, and on and on. What was I thinking?

When I went to his office a few days later, Tom's beautiful heavy Davek umbrella in hand, he generously insisted "No, keep it. I want you to have it." Every time I use that beautiful umbrella, I am reminded of two things.

First, what a fine person Tom is. Generous, approachable, humble. A servant leader, very different from many executives I have encountered over the years. And it brings home the point that kindness, at the end of the day, gets more followership and share of heart than being right and counting who gets what.

Even more, the umbrella reminds me of how much time and energy I spent worrying about what Tom would think about me. When, in reality, he probably never gave it a thought (that the quality of my umbrella was lower than his)...or if he did, it was fleeting at most.

Let's focus our energy on the important things.

Y is for Yeti – The Abominable Snowman of Negative Self-talk

The most successful among us may still have an unwanted, constant companion: The Yeti of Negative Self-talk.

Why do we waste so much of our lives wondering what other people will think about us? Why are we always the foolish ones, the wrong ones, the clueless ones, when things go wrong? Why is it so easy to put ourselves down? These are non-trivial questions. The next time the Yeti rears its ugly head, do two things.

One, re-frame *Yeti* into "It's really not that big a deal—*Yet*, I am blaming myself again!"

Two, discard your habitual self-blame by inserting the name of a friend or loved one.

If (insert your ally's name here) _____ had come to me with this story, would I have said "_____, how foolish of you?" "_____, what will people think about you?" "_____, you're a failure"? "_____ you can't do this"?

If the answer is (and in almost all cases, it will be) no, then remember: What could you achieve if you left the Yeti behind?

Reflect, for a moment, how much time and energy you have wasted in your life blaming yourself. Why do we allow ourselves to believe the silly names, the blame?[27] Let's take the advice instead of Grace Vanderwaal[28] and stand firm when malicious people try to knock us down: "I am not playing your game anymore. I am not clay."

Another solution to the Yeti syndrome is by removing the 'i' from the equation: how can you reframe the Yeti to 'not Yet'? I reference the work of the pioneering Dr. Carol Dweck[29], who talks of the power of positive use of the word 'yet'[30]. When someone says to themselves or to others: "This is hard, I can never do this," altering the response to "I don't know how to do this…*yet*" can change behavior significantly. This powerful tool is used with great purpose in a number of situations. The National Alliance for Partnerships in Equity (NAPE)[31] uses it to improve STEM[32] career success and teach students resilience, for example.

A similar tool that works for me is the word 'unless.' When you think "Getting my dream job is impossible" what happens when you add the word 'unless?' The sentence now reads "Getting my dream job is impossible unless…." And your brain starts unlocking solutions. "Unless I let my boss know that I want it." Or "Unless I speak to someone else who has that job about how she got there." You get the picture.

In order to free up time to achieve our mission, the next section will help us look at what we can stop doing.

Chapter 8

Behaviors That Get In The Way

This chapter focuses on the way we behave in self-destructive ways: the things we do that either waste time, or actually lead us away from our vision. First, we openly acknowledge what these projects, behaviors and tasks are, and then we stop doing them.

What will you *stop* doing?

Too often in life we try to stuff twenty pounds of activities into a six-pound bag. In order to get closer to our life goals, we have to stop doing something. It's simple math or science. Let's use a traffic analogy. If our car is constantly in the middle of a traffic jam, it will take way too long to get to our destination. Too many cars in front of us blocking our way. And a major accident or construction causes us to detour.

Data harvesting qualitative interviews with over a hundred people revealed an interesting pattern. Many of us live our entire lives on a detour track: waiting for the one day we will live our real life track. We say "this is my route until then," and then we stay on this bypass, until our life ends. Let's start removing the noise and traffic, so the path to our vision is unobstructed, or at least the traffic is light.

I divide the Stop Doing categories into *Projects, Tasks and Behaviors*. These three seemingly unrelated groupings get to the strategic, the tactical and the deeper interpersonal subtext. To summarize, let's analyze how much fluff there is in our lives, self-inflicted for the most part. We will analyze each area and decide which items to remove or reduce.

Stop Doing:

- Projects
- Tasks
- Behaviors

Let us go deeper into each of these areas.

Stop Doing Projects:

What are the major projects you are spending a lot of time and energy on? Now, while considering your own project list, be mindful of where you stand in Maslow's hierarchy of needs. Make sure basic financial needs are met, before you make drastic decisions: e.g. don't give up your only source of financial stability because it doesn't align with your vision. Establish a monetary stream which is aligned and sufficient first, then stop what is in the way of your true purpose. This category includes entire groups of things that no longer align with your vision.

Author's Note: I used to deliver leadership programs at organizations, using their materials. Transitioning to full-time writing and speaking about this book's topics forced me to re-evaluate time and resource allocation. As a result, I reluctantly discontinued these projects. It was work I enjoyed, paid the bills, matched my skill set; yet was not aligned with my purpose. Obviously a critical factor in this choice was that I could afford to do so.

Stop Doing Tasks:

What is the scenery of our lives? What are the things that fly by, that we don't notice, that impede or accelerate our progress? Think of the ride to work this week. What were the hundred or more billboards that flew by? Day after day, we perform tasks, some of them useful and valuable, some of them just a matter of habit. Do we filter out the noise that detracts from our life purpose? Media and social media is all pervasive in the current environment.

Let's talk about watching TV. How many hours do you spend watching inane television shows with false laughter tracks? Or gratuitous violence in a world where there are already too many senseless acts of anger and hatred?

Stop Doing Behaviors:

The Pareto Principle — also known as the 80/20 rule — applies here: reducing 20% of our unproductive behaviors can yield an 80% improvement in our productive free time. Obviously both percentages are arbitrary; the point of the Pareto Principle is that focusing on the critical few has significant impact.

Two behaviors to Stop Doing are:

- Saying yes to too many things.
- Staying in emotional danger zones.

It is important to find the root cause of why we say yes to too many things. Is it because we lack the courage to say no, or because saying yes fills a need in us? If we lack the courage to say no, let us practice the palatable truth techniques listed in chapter 3. If saying yes all the time fills a need, refer to the Five Whys methodology in chapter 6. Conduct your own Root Cause Analysis[33] in order to stop this behavior.

Assess the Danger Zones and Safe Spaces in Your Life:

a. Avoid or mitigate the danger zones.
b. Build safe spaces with intentionality.

Avoid or Mitigate Your Danger Zones:

This behavior has two aspects. First, recognizing the places where you have to be on guard; where you have to watch what you say, because there is a judge waiting to pounce on you. If you have a choice, reduce the time you spend feeling in danger. The second element of stopping this behavior is skilling up to protect yourself emotionally, while physically remaining in the danger zone, e.g. If we report to an emotionally unsafe boss, recognizing that we are in a danger zone is important. We can mitigate risk by using EQ skills like assertiveness and self-expression, to build a virtual buffer against her onslaughts.

Build your Safe Spaces:

- **List your Safe Spaces.** Places and people where stress is reduced. Your home, typically, will be your first safe space. Common additional examples may be family and friends' homes or neutral areas like a peaceful Starbucks. One can have virtual safe spaces also, such as a recurring phone call or Facetime with a loved one far away: where you can be yourself and re-energize.
- **Spend more time in the Safe Zones.** Some of this time is with the people on the top five list, and some is spent with others, or alone. It doesn't matter. Protect and nourish your quiet peace of mind.

Let's reconnect with our vision. Nietzsche said "He who has a why to live for can bear almost any how." If your vision is compelling enough, you will find the time to start doing that which moves you forward. First, stop doing enough things to clear up that time, then use it wisely. Obviously, there are many more behaviors than the two listed in that section. The purpose is to illustrate common ones and then have you identify your most unproductive behaviors.

Before you turn this page, make a note of actions to take, and what you will Stop Doing. What is the first step that you will take? For example, it will only take a few minutes to cancel the first Stop Doing item on your list. Review your options and pick an immediate action. Start this process which, while uncomfortable, at first, can save you time, energy and effort in the long run.

Stop Doing Projects Tasks and Behaviors

_____

_____

_____

_____

_____

_____

_____

_____

Danger Zone and Safe Spaces Listing and Actions

_____

_____

_____

_____

_____

_____

_____

Section Four:
Miserably Successful No More

This section synthesizes key lessons learned
into the final solution set:

L.I.G.H.T.E.N. U.P.

Let It Go / Handle Tension / Experience Now – Unleash your Power

We conclude with practical next steps and action planning.

Chapter 9

LIGHTEN UP - An Original Framework for Authentic Well-being

Together, we have gone through quite a journey, stopping our busy lives and taking inventory of ourselves. We have discovered our unique style, and reflected on who we are, where we want to go, and what we must stop doing in order to get there.

So, how shall we get there? When I share this framework in keynotes, the visual is of an ecstatic, beaming donkey, with huge shining teeth and a goofy smile: a perfect mental visual of *Lighten Up*. Take yourself and life less seriously, so you can achieve the important things. How does this idea relate to our collaborative success? In order for us to leverage our culture, race, religion, gender, and style (the focus of this book), we recognize our points of tension, handle them with maturity and humor, and unleash our power.

The L.I.G.H.T.E.N. U.P. Framework for Being Miserably Successful No More:

- *Let*
- *It*
- *Go!*

- *Handle*
- *Tension*

- *Experience*
- *Now*

- *Unleash (Your Authentic)*
- *Power*

Let's unpack the elements.

L.I.G. - Let It Go:

In order to let something go, we have to know what we are holding on to first. While this sounds simple it is difficult to execute. What has literally kept you awake at night? What is the nagging toothache of your mind? Who is the person that you squirm to be around, and have imaginary defensive arguments with, over and over again? What is the defeat that's bitter taste lingers in your mouth? What injustices have *they* inflicted on you — that unfair layoff, that crude comment, that passed over promotion, that meeting you weren't invited to?

It is not the thing or person itself that is the problem. It is your barnacle-like attachment to it. Again, in a spoken version of this concept, the visual is a hand holding a glass, with just a little water in it, with the tagline: *The longer you hold on to something, the heavier it gets.* I suggest you physically try this. Put some water in a regular sized glass or cup: it will feel light as you hold it strongly in the palm of your dominant hand. Do nothing. See how, in seconds, at most minutes, it is all you can think about: you will see, feel and be aware of nothing else. You are so afraid of dropping it that it takes over your mind.

The metaphor is a powerful one.

What is the *it* that you must let go?

Your response or emotions toward a person, an event or a thing.

_____

_____

_____

Why have you held on to it for so long?

_____

_____

_____

Who can help you let it go, if it's too hard to do it on your own?

_____

_____

_____

How will you measure your success in letting it go?

What is your plan to do so, starting right now?

Let's walk through some examples of what letting go can look like. For a person, the choices are letting go of the anger, or the connection itself, or the physical proximity. There is no right or wrong answer, just the one that works for you. I had a friend who I stayed connected with, even after we became very different people. After every phone call, there was a bitter taste in my mouth. Since the present relationship's negatives outweighed mildly fond memories of the past, this was a no brainer. Letting go meant simply severing all ties. It was easy, quick, relatively painless and freed up a large amount of 'BTUs'[34] for other, more fulfilling connections.

More difficult to let go was the sting associated with being laid off. That involved some introspection, because for a long time, my personal identity and self-worth had been associated with being this successful executive, that smart working person. And there was a practical financial sting as well, obviously. I know people who give away all corporate branded items of such organizations. Ironically, the act of physically letting go of these things may not cut the emotional hold: wearing a branded T-shirt of that company, could, in fact, be a sign that you have let it go.

> **What is the nagging toothache of your mind? What is the defeat that's bitter taste lingers in your mouth? It is not the thing itself that is the problem. It is your barnacle-like attachment to it.**

The point being, don't settle on the first, obvious answer. Honestly assess which are the two or three *its* that you need to let go. Imagine you are walking into the living room or den of your mind.

- *What* artifacts and curios make you angry?
- *Who* do you not want to see, sitting in your favorite chair?
- *How* will you get rid of them, so that the room of your mind is occupied by the critical few people and things that you cherish, learn and grow from and with?

You don't want this room to be cluttered, depressing or dirty. Clear out the cobwebs, throw out the trash. Politely say goodbye to that old relative who criticizes you while spilling red wine on your beautiful cream-colored sofa.

H.T. - Handle Tension:

We just completed an entire section on stressors. How to identify them, and which ones were holding you back. Hopefully, by now, you have several ideas of how to handle tension that will work for your unique personality and style.

Let's tie a bow on it by looking at three elements:

- *Analyze stressors*
- *Change the story*
- *What else might be true?*

Analyze Stressors

Go back to your top three stressors in chapter 6. Work toward reducing them.

Change The Story

By and large, we tend to inflate our own positives and downplay our negatives: the self-serving bias we looked at earlier. When I ask you to change the story, let me also remind you of the powerful question my mentor taught me: *"What else might be true?"*

What Else Might Be True?

When I was laid off, the first version of my story focused on the injustice of it, how unfair it was, who else was to blame. Years later, the story is completely different. While there may have been partial truths in my original story, asking 'what else might be true' allowed other facts to emerge. For example, that a number of people had been impacted by the layoff, not just me. That layoffs were often a numbers game, which I had logically understood when sitting at the other side of the table. Also, that the closing of this door had opened up a new world of possibilities. Ironically, being laid off was one of the best things that could have happened to me.

Understand your knee-jerk reaction. There may be value in it. Then step back and *change the story* by asking yourself *what else might be true*.

E.N. - Experience Now:

How often have you been in the middle of something that could, or should, have been amazing, and your brain was elsewhere? How often have you been stuck in the past, or so worried about the future that you could not enjoy the present? Mindfulness has become a popular buzz word these days. It applies to many actions in life: eating, breathing, thinking...

I was reminded of the irony, and challenge, of this approach recently when I found myself mentally checking off items from a 'to do list' in the middle of a massage. This massage had been scheduled to reduce tension before a hectic business trip. How absurd is that? We live in a world where multi-tasking has taken on a heroic flavor. Where we are praised for our super powers in juggling so many things at the same time. We proudly boast about it, almost like warriors comparing battle scars.

Working with Dr. Sandra Chapman's[35] team at the Center for Brain Health was an eye opener. She talks about the high cost of multi-tasking. And strongly advises us about the power of one — focusing on one thing at a time. One of her associates gave me a compelling metaphor for how this works. Imagine an automatic garage door opener. Every time we click that button on the remote, the garage door starts to open. Imagine if, mid-stride, we suddenly clicked it again, and the garage door stopped, then started working in the opposite direction. Then we clicked it again, and it stopped and started in the opposite direction again. After doing this hundreds of times, what would happen to the garage door? The obvious answer is: it would break down quickly.

And that, the brain health expert explained, is what happens to our brain under the stress of chronic multi-tasking. Our brain virtually 'opens and closes' every time we respond to an email, while taking an important phone call, and typing up the minutes of a meeting.

We gobble a sandwich while driving, *and* listen to an audio book at the same time: this is physically unhealthy *and* increases our stress. Some studies suggest that it can take up to ten minutes to shut down one task and reopen it effectively. While we think multi-tasking is efficient, it is, in reality, both ineffective and self-destructive. The smart thing to do, for both productivity and health, is to focus on one thing, complete it to the best of our abilities: and then start something else. Shut out distractions such as email alerts and ringing phones while completing it. If possible, set up separate chunks of time (refer to effective calendaring strategies listed in chapter 6) for routine tasks such as email and calls.

This advice is reinforced by Dr. Chozen Bays in *Mindful Eating*. She says that one of the best gifts of health we can give ourselves is to stop watching TV as we eat our dinner. She suggests that we slowly look at our food and actually taste it, and savor it. Were we to mindfully think of where it came from, and follow orioke (the ancient Japanese practice of just enough), we could reduce the epidemic of eating disorders, growing obesity and a host of related health issues.

Experience Now means: first decide what to do with this moment, that is not your right or due, but has been gifted to you. Ironically, the phone rang just as I was typing this sentence. Life is so strange sometimes, you can't make these things up.

A close family member called to invite me to go on an exciting outing, doing something I thoroughly enjoy. About to fall into the instant gratification pleasure trap, I asked if we could postpone our outing by a couple of hours. The <u>immediate and gracious</u> response "Of course!"

So I will go back to typing up this chapter (putting my phone on silent for the next two hours). Complete this section. Totally disengage my brain and try and connect the dots and make the framework come alive for you.

Having completed this wonderful, exhilarating experience of putting my thoughts down on paper, in a quiet, beautiful room, imagining you, reader, getting some value from the written words and ideas.

I commit to whole heartedly experiencing this perfect moment that has been gifted to me. *As J R R Tolkien said: "The only thing we have to decide is what to do with the time we have been given."*

Decide on one thing. Something that is valuable, that aligns with your vision, or increases yours or someone else's well-being. Then do it to the absolute best of your ability. Being IN that moment. And in no other. Doing THAT thing. And no other. *Try it. It just might change your entire life.*

U.P. - Unleash Power

Those of you who have read *Unleash the Power of Diversity*[36] will recognize the core concepts.

When we are truly ourselves, we can amaze ourselves with our authentic power. First, we have to understand our innate biases and destructive stereotypes about the limitations of people *in certain groups*. Next, we have to boldly shatter these tired culture, gender, style, generation and other stereotypes. First our own, then others'.

What does unleashing your authentic power look like?

- It looks like moving from being laid off, devastated, afraid to being blessed enough to touch thousands of people with one's written and spoken words.
- It looks like asking, "What would you do if you weren't afraid?" and then doing it.
- It looks like imagining something big. No, huge.
- And believing, truly believing, that you can achieve it.
- It looks like soaring.
- It looks like *"one moment in time[37], when I'm more than I thought I could be. When all of my dreams are a heartbeat away, and the answers are all up to me"*
  ~ Whitney Houston.

Please read this brilliant quote by Marianne Williamson once, quickly, then stop. Think about it. And then read it again slowly, and absorb it. *"Our deepest fear is not that we are inadequate. Our deepest fear is that we are powerful beyond measure."*

Conclusion and Action Planning

Let's look back at our journey together. We started out by asking:

- Who are you?
- What do you want out of your life?
- Where are you relative to your vision?

We then increased our self-awareness using multiple tools: Emotional Intelligence, Communication Styles, Behavioral Norms. We discovered surprising Style Biases and Stereotypes that were unique to our diverse personalities.

Next, we analyzed what makes us miserably successful, taking a deeper dive into major stressors. We introduced easy to remember acronyms for M.I.S.E.R.Y. and S.T.R.E.S.S.; synthesizing years of data collection into actionable insights.

We looked at ways to reduce our stress, and a logical approach for us to Stop Doing certain tasks, projects and behaviors.

Finally, we put it all together with the original 'L.I.G.H.T.E.N. U.P.' framework: Let It Go, Handle Tension, Experience Now; Unleash Authentic Power.

Action Planning

Now it is time for us to design specific actions to implement the book's learning.

- What is one thing that you will start doing, as a result of reading this book?
- One thing that you will stop doing?
- What is the most important idea or thought that will stay with you?

_____

_____

_____

_____

_____

_____

_____

_____

_____

_____

_____

_____

_____

_____

_____

Thank you for your support through this journey of reflection, self-discovery, and call to action. If this book has been of value to you, please pay it forward.

I close with a stanza from the brilliant David Whyte. He talked about the popular pilgrimage to Camino De Santiago in Spain. When pilgrims reach the end of their journey at the water's edge, many take off the boots that served them so well in the past. And put on a new pair of shoes for this next path forward.

What will your new shoes look like?

What are the boots that have served you well, and are no longer needed?

How will you discard them, to make space for your new path?

Travel with me across the miles, and imagine David Whyte himself, sharing his powerful poem with us:

FINISTERRE

The road in the end taking the path the sun had taken,
into the western sea, and the moon rising behind you
as you stood where ground turned to ocean: no way
to your future now but the way your shadow could take,
walking before you across water, going where shadows go,
no way to make sense of a world that wouldn't let you pass
except to call an end to the way you had come,
to take out each frayed letter you had brought
and light their illumined corners; and to read
them as they drifted on the late western light;
to empty your bags; to sort this and to leave that;
to promise what you needed to promise all along,
and to abandon the shoes that brought you here
right at the water's edge, not because you had given up
but because now, you would find a different way to tread,
and because, through it all, part of you would still walk on,
no matter how, over the waves.

~ David Whyte
from *Pilgrim*
©2014 Many Rivers Press

I see you. You are as me, caught in what Covey called the thick of thin things. Take a deep breath, as I did a moment ago[38].

There is no moment in time but this one, fleeting and ephemeral, powerful in its fragility.

Together, shall we seize this moment, and, gathering momentum, make it momentous?

All movements start with a single, small step. What will yours be?

Debjani Mukherjee Biswas

Appendix

Notes Pages

_____

_____

_____

_____

_____

_____

_____

_____

_____

_____

_____

_____

_____

_____

_____

_____

_____

_____

_____

_____

Notes Pages

_____

_____

_____

_____

_____

_____

_____

_____

_____

_____

_____

_____

_____

_____

_____

_____

_____

_____

_____

_____

_____

_____

M is for Materialism Checklist

Also useful for assessing clutter causing stress

My home or apartment is too big, too small, just right	B S R
My car is too expensive, too cheap, just right	E C R
(if you are in a family where two or more people share two or more cars, rate each one) Car 2	E C R
My TV or Audio system is too expensive, too cheap, just right	E C R
The number of clothes I own are too many, too few, just right	M F R
The number of shoes I own are too many, too few, just right	M F R
Overall my home's decorating style is cluttered, empty, just right	C E R
The number of books in my house is too high, too low, just right	H L R
The sports equipment number is too high, too low, just right	H L R
The number of suitcases is too high too low, just right	H L R
The number of decorative items is too high, too low, just right	H L R
The number of pots and pans is too high, too low, just right	H L R
The number of sheets (bed linen) is too high, too low, just right	H L R
The number of towels (bathroom) is too high, too low, just right	H L R
The number of toiletries (makeup, soap, hotel shampoos, lotions, shaving items) is too high, too low, just right	H L R
The number of _____ (insert what else you own here) is too high, too low, just right	H L R
My office is too cluttered, too sparse, just right	C S R
My car is too cluttered, too empty, just right	C E R
The number of _____ (insert what else you own here) is too high too low just right	H L R
The number of _____ (insert what else you own here) is too high too low just right	H L R
The number of _____ (insert what else you own here) is too high too low just right	H L R
The number of _____ (insert what else you own here) is too high too low just right	H L R
The number of _____ (insert what else you own here) is too high too low just right	H L R

Distinguishing Markers

Self-assessment of top 3-5

_____

_____

_____

_____

Others' assessment of top 3-5

_____

_____

_____

_____

Surprises, if any

_____

_____

_____

_____

_____

How will you improve your Distinguishing Markers while remaining authentic?

_____

_____

_____

_____

Three-Legged Stool

Practical

_____

_____

_____

_____

_____

External

_____

_____

_____

_____

Internal

_____

_____

_____

_____

_____

Style Norms and Biases

Please circle or fill in the blank with the most accurate answer

If you are uncomfortable documenting your responses, mentally answer the questions and process the learning internally.

- I would be _____ happy, embarrassed, relieved, OK either way (circle one or insert word here) if I were married to/dating a really chatty person.

  - This is because: _____

    _____

    _____

    _____

- I _____ dislike/appreciate/admire/am curious about (circle one or insert word here) people who speak up for themselves, even if their viewpoint is controversial or against the majority opinion.

  - This is because: _____

    _____

    _____

    _____

- I feel _____ impressed by/uncomfortable around/ irritated by (circle one or insert word) people who are always well dressed and well groomed.

  - This is because: _____

    _____

_____

_____

- If I walked into a party with a large group of strangers and a few people I know, I would be _____ intimidated/ exhilarated/neutral (circle one or insert word here).

  • This is because: _____

  _____

  _____

  _____

- I connect most with people who are _____ (age, culture, style, gender descriptor).

  • This is because: _____

  _____

  _____

  _____

- Being late for a lunch appointment with a close friend is _____not a big deal, rude, embarrassing (circle one or insert word).

  • This is because: _____

  _____

  _____

  _____

- I am annoyed by people who are/do/say

  _____ (behavioral characteristic).

  • This is because: _____

  _____

  _____

  _____

Behavioral beliefs are learned in childhood or developed through personal experiences as an adult. They could be positive or negative traits about people around you.

Some of my behavioral beliefs about my peers and those around me are:

_____

_____

_____

_____

_____

_____

_____

_____

Stop Doing Projects Tasks and Behaviors

_____

_____

_____

_____

_____

_____

_____

Danger Zone and Safe Spaces Listing and Actions

_____

_____

_____

_____

_____

_____

_____

Meet the Author

Mukherjee Biswas' vision is 'learning, helping, teaching — with graceful, flawed authenticity.' This journey began with the unconditional support of her parents Reba and Debu Mukherjee. They boldly shattered tired gender and cultural stereotypes, to ensure unlimited access to the career and life of her choice. She is also deeply grateful to family and friends for their unwavering belief in her.

The author graduated with a Bachelor's in Chemical Engineering from IIT (Indian Institute of Technology) Madras, receiving the Institute Gold Medal for outstanding contributions. After an MBA in Marketing at IIM (Indian Institute of Management) Bangalore, she worked at the Tata Administrative Services.

Moving to the U.S., Ms. Biswas received a second Master's in Organizational Strategy and International Management; and a Professional & Executive Coaching certification — both from the University of Texas at Dallas. She went on to become a certified Emotional Intelligence, Myers-Briggs, Firo B and Thomas-Kilmann practitioner. An active volunteer and STEM Advocate, she serves on the Board of Directors of her engineering alumni organization IIT North Texas.

After two decades of managerial and executive experience in corporate America (Texas Instruments, PepsiCo), Ms. Biswas changed career paths in 2012. She is currently an international keynote speaker, change agent and President of Coachieve, LLC (Leadership and Diversity Strategies). Her first book, *Unleash the Power of Diversity*, was selected by Barnes & Noble for in-store presence. Ms. Biswas completed a U.S. Barnes & Noble book tour in 2014.

Mukherjee Biswas' third book *A Power Paradox* is forthcoming.

Please write a review of this book on Amazon. Your feedback is valuable to us.

To give us your feedback or contact us for keynotes and workshops please email contact@coachieve.us

Also by Debjani Mukherjee Biswas

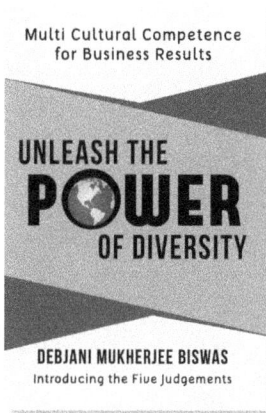

Multi Cultural Competence
for Business Results

UNLEASH THE
P◉WER
OF DIVERSITY

DEBJANI MUKHERJEE BISWAS
Introducing the Five Judgements

In her first book in the Power Leadership Series, Mukherjee Biswas examines the connection between business results and multicultural competence. Her groundbreaking stereotyping and framework "The Five Judgments" received widespread positive responses when introduced in 2013. They explore how our hidden biases about others and, surprisingly, ourselves, impact business success and power. Available on Amazon and a Barnes & Noble in-store selection.

The Five Judgments© - Business Costs of Stereotyping

- Reputational Currency – Buzz
- Physical Impact – Visual
- Auditory Cues – Sound
- Distinguishing Markers© – Differentiators
- Work Product - Output

A Diversity Foray - Global Toolkit for Multicultural Competence

Do	Don't
Ask	Shun
Accept	Patronize
	Assume
Adapt	Crumble
Appreciate	Escalate

www.ingramcontent.com/pod-product-compliance
Lightning Source LLC
Chambersburg PA
CBHW051723260326
41914CB00031B/1701/J